THE CPO

TRANSFORMING PROCUREMENT
IN THE REAL WORLD

Christian Schuh

Michael F. Strohmer

Stephen Easton

Armin Scharlach

Peter Scharbert

Illustrations by Tomaž Nečemar

Apress®

The CPO: Transforming Procurement in the Real World

ISBN-13 (pbk): 978-1-4302-4962-7

ISBN-13 (electronic): 978-1-4302-4963-4

President and Publisher: Paul Manning

Lead Editor: Jeff Olson

Editorial Board: Steve Anglin, Mark Beckner, Ewan Buckingham, Gary Cornell, Louise Corrigan, Morgan Ertel, Jonathan Gennick, Jonathan Hassell, Robert Hutchinson, Michelle Lowman, James Markham, Matthew Moodie, Jeff Olson, Jeffrey Pepper, Douglas Pundick, Ben Renow-Clarke, Dominic Shakeshaft, Gwenan Spearing, Matt Wade, Tom Welsh

Coordinating Editor: Rita Fernando

Copy Editor: Deanna Hegle

Compositor: Bytheway Publishing Services

Art Processing: SPi Global

Cover Designer: Anna Ishchenko

Distributed to the book trade worldwide by Springer Science+Business Media New York, 233 Spring Street, 6th Floor, New York, NY 10013. Phone 1-800-SPRINGER, fax (201) 348-4505, e-mail orders-ny@springer-sbm.com, or visit www.springeronline.com. Apress Media, LLC is a California LLC and the sole member (owner) is Springer Science + Business Media Finance Inc (SSBM Finance Inc). SSBM Finance Inc is a Delaware corporation.

For information on translations, please e-mail rights@apress.com, or visit www.apress.com.

Apress and friends of ED books may be purchased in bulk for academic, corporate, or promotional use. eBook versions and licenses are also available for most titles. For more information, reference our Special Bulk Sales–eBook Licensing web page at www.apress.com/bulk-sales.

This Book Is Dedicated to Our Clients

Contents

About the Authors

The five authors work for A.T. Kearney and have been with the firm for ten to twenty years.

Christian Schuh has led procurement transformation projects for clients in the automotive, construction equipment, defense, high tech, packaging, and steel industry in Europe, Russia, China, and the USA. He is the author of various books on procurement (most notably *The Purchasing Chessboard*), monographs, and articles. Christian studied aeronautical engineering at TU Graz and holds a doctorate in business administration. He lives in the historic city center of Vienna.

Michael F. Strohmer is an expert on raw material strategies, procurement transformation, post-merger management, and large-scale CAPEX projects. His work encompasses the utilities sector, automotive, defense, consumer goods, packaging, and steel. He has published several books (including *The Purchasing Chessboard*) and articles, and he is a frequent speaker at international conferences. Michael holds doctorate degrees in business administration and law. He lives in Austria's picturesque lake region near Salzburg.

Stephen Easton is a specialist on improving the effectiveness of external procurement activities. He has supported a number of both private and public sector clients to achieve significant and sustained financial results. Stephen has an MBA from Cornell University and a first degree in Politics, Philosophy, and Economics from the University of Oxford. He lives in Surrey, southwest of London.

Armin Scharlach is helping clients around the world in transformation projects to define holistic procurement IT architectures. He is also a recognized thought leader in advanced collaborative approaches, helping CPOs to find additional savings when the low-hanging fruit has been collected already. With his innovative, high-end analytics, he is breaking through the barriers of traditional procurement and supply chain methods. Armin lives in Berlin.

Peter Scharbert has led numerous procurement-related projects in Europe and in the Middle East for clients from various industries, including pharmaceutical/life sciences, financial services, and diversified conglomerates. His specific focus is on procurement performance management, procurement transformation, and strategic sourcing. Peter holds a degree in industrial engineering from University of Karlsruhe. He lives in the Basel area, where Switzerland, France, and Germany meet.

Acknowledgments

Following the sequence of events, we would like to thank:

Martina Bihn from Springer for getting us on the radar screen of Apress.

Rebecca Raudabaugh for converging the styles of five authors (four of which are non English native speakers!) into a legible text that convinced Apress to publish us.

Jeff Olson for having faith in us and dedicating countless hours to turning our manuscript into an actual book.

Alenka Triplat for introducing Tomaž Nečemar to us.

Tomaž Nečemar for visualizing our ideas.

Prologue

My name is Thomas Sutter. I'm 37 years old. I grew up on the Rhein-Main U.S./NATO air base in Frankfurt, Germany. My father, an American, was a pilot during Operation Desert Storm, also known as the Gulf War. My mother, from Frankfurt, met my father on a visit to the base. Though I grew up on the base, I spent a lot of time off the base with my mother's family in Frankfurt and felt more German than American. When the "purebred" American kids were playing Little League baseball on the base, I was taking violin lessons in the city or visiting the Städel Museum to view the art of the Old Masters. Much to my father's chagrin, I went to the gymnasium in Frankfurt rather than the base high school, and then off to the Technische Universität in Berlin.

My parents moved back to the States in the late 1990s and now live in Chicago, but it should be no surprise that I stayed in Germany. I live in Dusseldorf, working nearby in Essen for the global car manufacturer, Autowerke AG, as the Group Commodity Manager of Electrics/Electronics, part of the procurement department. For the last few months, I've been immersed in automotive entertainment devices. Competition in the auto industry is tough, and we want to not just "keep up with the Joneses" but lead the way in offering innovative devices for automobiles. Our new in-car entertainment system—we call it ICE—is still on the drawing boards as we assess supply and demand power: That's how much power we have as buyers, and how much power the suppliers have, to negotiate price, features, and so forth.

Our procurement policies are, if I do say so myself, world class. Not long ago, we reduced costs by 10%. In one year. Across the *entire* company. Just so no one thought it was a fluke, we reduced costs an additional 7.3% the following year. Those kinds of yearly reductions are not sustainable, of course, but our methods have given our competitors fits. "How can they offer that automobile for that price?," they wonder. Naturally, manufacturing and engineering processes improved in tandem with our results, but I'll say it again: Our procurement methods—forecasting, scouting and sourcing, negotiating, tracking, helping vendors improve, managing the supply chain, and so on—are the best in the world. They have to be, considering how commodity prices rise and fall (but mostly rise) from year to year. We also have some of the best minds in the company working in procurement, including my mentor, Dan Schaeffler, Autowerke's CPO [Chief Procurement Officer], who has guided my career at the company from the start.

Most important, we work together. There's no "silo mentality" at Autowerke—collaboration is key to our success. Some of my closest colleagues are, for example, in engineering. Procurement, we've known for some time now, must work closely with all the company's functions to produce the best results.

It's not an easy job, but it is one I relish—even when I'm on the phone with China at dawn or the United States late at night. It engages all my training, my experience, and my interests. To relieve the stress, I recently took up running.

My wife is Heidi Sutter. She is German and the mother of our two children, Johanna, seven, and David, five. A lawyer, she is on the fast track to partner at her law firm. Our full-time, demanding jobs led us to employ a full-time nanny, Ekaterina, who is also teaching the children her native Russian.

Like most Germans, I work long hours. Heidi does as well, but she has a particular fear—that I will put my job ahead of hers. That's exactly what happened to Heidi's sister, and the marriage ended up on the rocks. She is adamant the same thing won't happen to her, yet she knows I'm the restless sort, always on the lookout for a new challenge.

I am now off to California to talk to Greenway Electronics, one of the biggest electronics device makers in the world, and which has taken over the entire smartphone market with its signature products. As big as Autowerke is, Greenway is just as big and looms larger in the public mind. Any deal we make will have to be win–win and a partnership of equals.

I will be stopping in Chicago first to see my parents.

What is taking you to Chicago?

I soon discover that I won't be watching a movie or sleeping on this flight. An hour in, I've learned that Ross is the CEO of Heartland Consolidated Industries, Inc., the consumer goods giant. That is why he looked familiar.

Slowly, the conversation shifts to Thomas's career and responsibilities at Autowerke.

So this is how you save billions today.

Thomas let me tell you something. I am really intrigued by what you are telling me and even more by how you are telling it.

Well, believe me, we have not stood still over the past decades.

We at Heartland could use someone like you. Before you say anything, let me make a suggestion . . .

I still remember hanging out at the air base—my father served with the 435th Tactical Airlift Wing at the Rhein-Main—where everyone had been friendly and even turned a blind eye whenever Dad would take me on the C-5 Galaxy he piloted. Not only did he pilot one of the largest aircraft in the world, but he was even decorated for his heroics in Operation Desert Storm. Despite practically growing up at the Frankfurt airport, I hate what it has become.

The airport of my childhood had been an easy affair, and relatively small. Now I have to run to the International Terminal in what seems like an endless underground tunnel. On the moving walkway, families with lots of luggage are blocking the way and my delayed flight from Düsseldorf cut ten minutes off my connection time. It is 7:42, and my flight to Chicago leaves at 8:10. Glancing at one of the monitors, the status jumps from "boarding" to "gate closing." I might be able to get onto the 10:35 flight if I miss this one, but I want to spend as much time with my parents as possible—I don't get over there enough.

Panting, I finally make it to the check-in counter. A smiling gate agent greets me: "Good morning Mr. Sutter, we've been waiting for you. Today's flight is overbooked in Business Class, so we have taken the liberty of upgrading you to First Class." This is a pleasant surprise after waking up at four to catch my flight out of Dusseldorf.

I've made a habit of introducing myself to my seatmate on the plane, as opposed to just plopping down in the seat as if they don't exist. People tend to be startled by the pleasantries, but it usually makes plane rides more agreeable in general. As I walk through the jetway and into first class, I find my seat. I can't help but notice how the muscular man in his mid-sixties, occupying the seat next to mine, radiates an aura of power and confidence. Although the type is familiar—I've met many such men in the Autowerke boardroom when I've gone there to give a presentation—I am not sure they make the best flying companions. I wonder why he is not using a corporate jet.

I decide it doesn't matter. He's there, so I go through my routine: "Hi, I'm Thomas Sutter, do you mind if I put my bag here in between our seats?" The other passenger looks up from the Financial Times and gives me a head to toe once-over.

Then he extends his beefy hand. "Of course not. I'm Ross, Ross Bailkowsky, nice to meet you. What is taking you to Chicago?"

I soon discover that I won't be watching a movie or sleeping on this flight. An hour in, I've learned that Ross is the CEO of Heartland Consolidated Industries, Inc., the consumer goods giant. That is why he looked familiar, I think, as I remember what I know about the company. Heartland has recently won a bidding war for a dairy company in Bavaria that attracted quite a lot of media attention in Germany. Ross tells me he grew up on a farm in Montana and has never forgotten his humble beginnings. He seldom takes the corporate jet.

Ross is a great plane buddy—jovial and with a good sense of humor, he's taken an interest in my binational upbringing. Ross's younger brother was in the U.S. Air Force, so we discuss the various aspects of military life. I tell him that I mainly remember having fun pushing the buttons. Slowly, the conversation shifts to my job at Autowerke. Ross is simply being polite in asking about my work. But then I mention the €4 billion Autowerke's procurement department has saved the company in each of the previous five years, and he starts to quiz me. "How?" he asks simply.

I launch into the well-rehearsed speech I usually give when recruiting talent at universities. "You know, Autowerke really started professional procurement. It was back in 1985, when our CEO decided that something drastic needed to be done to counter the challenge posed by Japanese carmakers. He took a long hard look at all the disciplines in Autowerke and spotted the one that really was underperforming—procurement. He put an aspiring young plant manager from Italy, Giacomo Venier, in charge and tasked him with saving one billion deutschmarks. The first thing Giacomo did was swap responsibilities among buyers. By breaking up long-established relationships, he saved the first 5%." I notice with some surprise that Ross has started taking notes.

I continue. "What Giacomo did next was use the global supply market. He did this in a very smart way. At first, he showed people a chart that had the share of purchases a plant did in the country where it was based. Guess what the lowest share of local purchasing was? 95%! The German plants were exclusively buying in Germany, the Italian plants in Italy, and so on. He then incentivized procurement people to do two things: first, to use suppliers from other countries and second, to convince peers from other countries to use their suppliers. Within two years, he had brought down the average share of local suppliers to 85%. So, as I said before, Autowerke really was the first big corporation to bring procurement into the boardroom. All the other carmakers followed our example, and we have influenced many other industries as well."

Ross is incredulous. "So this is how you save billions today, by swapping responsibilities and sharing suppliers? I can see how this helps at first, but surely the effect must wear off over time."

I continue my business school speech. "Well, believe me, we have not stood still over the past decades. By now, we have a very sophisticated approach to reducing cost and increasing value with suppliers. We base all our actions on a profound understanding of supply power and demand power."

"Supply and demand is hardly a new concept," Ross observes. "I learned about it in Econ 101."

"You're right there," I retort with a smile. "The question is what you make of it. We use it to come up with very differentiated approaches when dealing with suppliers. Let me give you a couple of examples. Take forgings. Autowerke is one of the world's largest buyers of forgings, so we enjoy very high demand power. At the same time, there are hundreds of forges out there that can fulfill our demand, so they have very low supply power. In such a scenario, we don't even bother to do the requests for proposals. What we do instead is collect specifications and prices from all the forged parts we have globally. We then put all of this data into a statistical tool that determines target prices we impose on our suppliers."

"What if a supplier doesn't agree to that target price?" Ross asks.

"Not a good idea. Remember, there are hundreds of qualified alternatives out there. If a supplier doesn't comply with what we consider a fair and competitive price, the supplier gets replaced. But this hardly happens. Actually, we have evidence that our continuous price pressure is helping suppliers to become more competitive than their peers who are not working with us. We pride ourselves in having had a major role in helping the overall European automotive industry to weather the challenge of Japanese carmakers in the eighties and nineties. Sadly, we are just a niche player in the U.S.—only 2% of the market—so our influence there is limited."

"Yeah, I can relate to that. You know, I still buy American when it comes to cars. But what Detroit has come up with over the past 30 years isn't really attractive. When I was a kid, American cars were fantastic, powerful, and beautiful machines. My first car was a 1963 Mustang, black with red seats. I bought it with the money I made fixing farm equipment all over the area. But what about this statistical tool of yours—would it also work at a company like Heartland Consolidated Industries?"

I pause, wondering how much to tell him. Something about him encourages my trust, so I decide to continue. "Where Heartland has high demand power and is facing suppliers with low supply power, it would absolutely work. But it would not work in other scenarios. Let me give you another example from Autowerke. Depending on how you look at the global car market, we are number one or number two, so we have a very high demand power for things like engine management systems, right? But the thing is, there are only three suppliers out there that are seriously in that technology. And when it comes to our specifics, it really is just one that can fulfill our demand. Guess what would happen if we tried to impose target prices on them?"

Ross snorted. "They would tell you to get lost."

"Well maybe not such a harsh response, because they need us as much as we need them. But we would suffer, for sure. They would gradually start to divert attention to our competitors. We wouldn't get their latest innovations and lose competitiveness in the market. So we are very much into nurturing a partnership with them. There is a continuous dialogue between our CEO and their CEO, our head of engineering and their head of engineering, and so on. The object of all these conversations is to perfectly align innovation cycles.

generation to best benefit both parties."

Ross looks thoughtful. "Interesting. I'm trying to remember when I have met one of Heartland's suppliers. Hmm, must be ages. I do meet customers all the time, however."

"Well, yours is a very different industry, but I'm sure there must be suppliers that are crucial for your success in the market."

"You're probably right there. But you know what, it would take me a while to figure out who to ask. We don't have a proper supply management or procurement function at group level. I think all of this is done at the division or even business-unit level."

I've been so into my spiel of explaining the fine points of Autowerke's approach that I had not noticed the change in Ross's posture. Ross has shifted the bulk of his weight in a way that allows him to face me as much as physically possible in an airplane seat. He has all but forgotten about the light lunch on the tray in front of him, and he is fully absorbing my comments.

I continue. "Let me give you another example. Even a company as large as Autowerke can find itself in a situation where low demand power is facing high supply power. This is the most inconvenient situation you can find yourself in. Right now, we're having a problem with platinum. Platinum is used in catalytic converters. Our demand is a fraction of the world market and the price level is determined at the London Metal Exchange. So because we cannot influence the price we pay at all, the way forward is to engineer ourselves out of platinum. We have very promising alternative catalytic converters in the pipeline."

"Looks like you guys are way ahead of anything we do at Heartland," Ross frowns. Then he laughs. "I bet your ticket was cheaper than mine, too."

"Apart from you paying for First Class while I got an upgrade, not necessarily. You know, Heartland Consolidated and Autowerke may be big companies; but they are still only one of many customers traveling with United and Lufthansa. This is the scenario in which low demand power meets low supply power. Sometimes we do better, and sometimes they do better depending on specific situations. And yes, we do negotiate a price with the airlines, but the main lever is avoiding business flights altogether. At Autowerke we have a very sophisticated videoconferencing system. We are cutting the number of flights we do annually at an astonishing rate."

Ross eyes me closely. "So this flight must have an important reason then."

"Yes it does, I'm going to meet a high-tech company in the Bay Area for what I expect to be a major breakthrough." Ross has the courtesy not to quiz me further on the exact reasoning of my trip to the United States. He remains silent for a while. Then he speaks.

"Thomas, let me tell you something. I am really intrigued by what you are telling me and even more by how you are telling it. I can sense you have a lot of energy and drive. Heartland Consolidated Industries needs someone like you. Before you say anything, let me make a suggestion. Tomorrow a couple of my associates from Heartland will join me at the country club in Fort Wayne for golf. Why don't you join us there? I can arrange for a jet to pick you up in Chicago and take you back as well. Do you think your parents would mind not having you there on Sunday?"

After a short hesitation, I agree. My dad has always encouraged me to go for opportunities. Although I'm pretty sure I'm not going to leave Autowerke, it is flattering for one of the world's most prestigious executives to take an interest in me.

CPO Best Practices

- Base your purchasing strategies on an understanding of supply and demand power for each category of item you buy.

- Remember that the full value of vendor relationships goes beyond price to include innovation and service.

- However, avoid cozy procurement/vendor relationships in which the value is not understood and there is no creative tension in the relationship.

Chapter 2:
Sunday Night
Back in Chicago

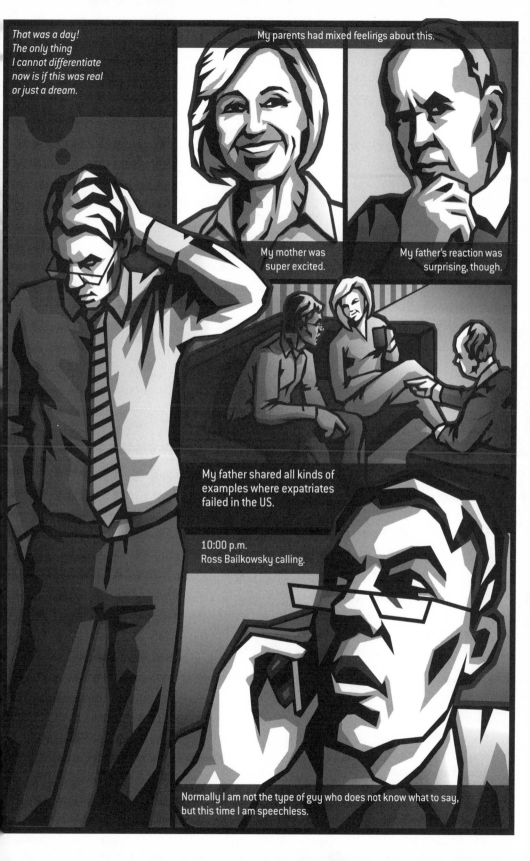

What a day! I almost feel the need to pinch myself to make sure it really happened. Ross and his associates are very nice—Ross truly cares, and it shows. It must be weird to have a personal assistant shadow you around all day—following up on every detail Ross says, even on the golf course. Although everyone was welcoming, I rode an emotional roller coaster all day. Being a part of the crowd is fun, but it also feels a little artificial. Listening to a conversation in my head, I chuckle as I hear Dad telling me I have "gone native" in Europe. And maybe it is true. At Autowerke nobody would be as overwhelming and open as all the guys are here—and I'm not sure what I like more.

I did quite like John, who heads Marketing. He understands European culture well—his grandfather emigrated from Italy in the 1920s, and he goes back quite a bit. We discovered that his family comes from the same village where Heidi and I like to go on vacation. John also tries to go back to Italy every year to visit his distant cousins—his kids enjoy the culture, countryside, and food there. I mentioned a small trattoria called Leo's, which we love. It's the kind of place you wouldn't know if you didn't really know the village, and it serves the best coniglio in vino bianco con rosmarino—rabbit in white wine with rosemary—I've ever had. Turns out this trattoria belongs to one of his relatives! Heidi and I once spent a day there attending a cooking class on real Italian dishes. The world really is quite small.

I didn't see a lot of Fort Wayne itself, just the airport I flew into and the country club where we spent the day. Amazing—I never thought I would be picked up by a private jet just to play golf. I'm still thinking about what Ross and I talked about today. After inviting me into the clubhouse in a separate room, offering me a cigar (I do not smoke) and a whiskey (at one in the afternoon!), I started to feel like a mob boss.

Ross told me that he was quite impressed by our conversation on the plane, and then he dropped the bombshell: He offered me a job—to become the first chief procurement officer (CPO) of Heartland Consolidated Industries. CPO! This would be a huge step. To become CPO at Autowerke—if it ever happened—would take at least another five or seven years. And yet I got a personal offer from Heartland's CEO.

I'd be lying if I said I wasn't thinking about it.

I was surprised my parents had mixed feelings about this. I assumed they would be ecstatic to see Heidi, the kids, and me move to the United States. Mom was beaming at the thought of her grandkids being so much closer. She really misses me, her only son, who is so far away, and especially misses seeing the grandkids every now and then. Johanna and David sometimes complain too that their friends have their grandparents much closer and can see them almost every day.

My father's reaction was surprising, however. Even though it would be a major step in my career, Dad was cautious. "You don't know what you are getting into Thomas—this is a completely different industry. And U.S. firms have a different culture than Europe." He also reminded me that it had been a dream of mine to work at Autowerke ever since I was ten years old. My father then shared examples of expatriates failing in the United States. All good points, but still … CPO! What if I stay at Autowerke and the promotions stop happening? I'd always regret not taking this job. It hurts that Dad isn't encouraging me to go after an opportunity like this.

An then there's Heidi—she pops into my head yet again. She will not be happy with this. Either we would have to move to the United States jointly, or I could probably negotiate with Ross that I go home to Dusseldorf every other weekend. But Heidi would never agree to that. And besides, her career is on the upswing. When she hears about this she'll think first about her sister and the sacrifices she made for her lousy husband and his career before he left her.

It's 10 p.m. here in Chicago. I am drowsy and jet-lagged. My mobile phone rings, slamming me back into reality. Who is calling me at this time of night? The display reads Ross Bailkowsky. I answer, and he mentions that he is in his office to sort out some things. I heard this afternoon that it's one of his habits to go to the office Sunday evening and prepare for the week ahead.

"Thomas, I just talked to our president and some of the other board members. I have a green light to offer you total compensation of $650,000 with a guaranteed bonus that'll bring it close to $750,000 in the first year. Additionally, there will be full health care for your family, housing paid for the first six months until you find a home to buy, and you and your family will get four personal flights to Europe every year. So, think about it and call me once you've made up your mind." He hangs up before I have a chance to respond. I couldn't have spoken anyway. Ross stunned me into silence. The CPO job— with well over twice the money I'm making now at Autowerke! I stare out my window, imagining my future.

Chapter 3:
Late Night Phone Call to Heidi

I have been lying in bed for what feels like years. Maybe even a lifetime. I've tossed and turned to the point where I have a sheet cobra-wrapped around my right leg, inhibiting blood flow. CPO of Heartland Consolidated Industries. Fort Wayne. My impending Greenway Electronics meeting. Heidi. Autowerke. The kids. I sit up, no longer able to pretend I'm asleep. Looking at the red LED glow of the clock, I put my glasses on and see it's after midnight, meaning it's past 7:00 a.m. in Dusseldorf—Heidi is up. Before I think it through, I am dialing our home phone.

"Hi Thomas," Heidi answers. "It's a bit late there. I thought you would be asleep already for the big meeting."

"Hi, I can't sleep. Can we talk?" I ask.

"Sure, I'm getting ready for work," Heidi says. "Let me put you on speaker. Ekaterina is getting the kids ready for school. I need to say goodbye. Why can't you sleep?"

"There is too much going on. I was offered a job yesterday."

"What?"

In my mind I can see Heidi practically dropping the phone.

"I met a man on the plane, we played golf this afternoon, and he offered me a job."

"You what ... hang on, yes, bye, bye, mommy loves you ... yes, no, I am talking to Daddy.... Thomas, the children want to say hello," Heidi says, flustered by the bomb I just dropped.

"Great," I answer.

"Hello Daddy," say Johanna and David in unison.

"Have a good day at school!" I tell them. There is a pause as I hear Ekaterina coming to collect the children for school.

"This sounds like something out of a spy novel. You met a man on a plane and he offered you a job?"

"Yes."

"Who was the man and what is the job?"

"His name is Ross Bailkowsky, he is the President of Heartland Consolidated Industries, a huge U.S. company, and the job is to be the new CPO."

Heidi is silent for a moment, then says, "I can't believe this. But I guess I should congratulate you. Where would this job be?"

"Fort Wayne," I reply.

"That doesn't help. Where is that?"

"Indiana."

"That's in the middle of nowhere isn't it? They even have their own time zone, don't they?"

"Indiana is quite nice," I say, "a good environment for children. I've already been out to Fort Wayne. It's a nice town."

"So is Dusseldorf," says Heidi. "Wait, you've already been there? I'm confused."

"Yes, I went this afternoon in Ross's jet and played golf."

"This is even more like a spy novel," says Heidi. "You're becoming quite the jet-setter ..."

"Things happened very quickly yesterday."

"I'll say. What about me? Where do the kids and I fit in? I bet my firm doesn't have an office in Fort Wayne. This all sounds really serious."

"That's why I had to talk to you my love," I say. "I can't sleep thinking about it. It does sound interesting, and it would be a big increase in responsibility. I'll be running my own show at last. Think of that."

"But, it would be a big change for us as a family," says Heidi.

"I know ... I needed to talk to you about it." I pull my ace out. "They'd be paying me almost $750,000."

"That won't make us any happier," she says immediately. "But yes, we need to talk," Heidi agrees. "I can't take this all in at once. Job offers on planes, private jets, Fort Wayne ... and here I am in Dusseldorf trying to get ready for work. I have a major client meeting at nine. This is really not a good time, Thomas Sutter."

Heidi only uses my full name when she's unhappy. Suddenly my brain kicks in as I realize I crossed a boundary this early in the morning. A rushed phone call on speaker while Heidi is getting ready for work is not the most tactful way to have this conversation. But if I had waited until I got home she probably would have been upset as well. It's a lose–lose situation no matter how I handled it.

"Can we talk later?" I ask.

"When?"

"Tonight."

"Maybe," Heidi says. "Thomas, I really need to get to work."

"Ok. I love you."

"We'll talk later," Heidi says pointedly, and the phone goes dead.

Chapter 4:
Advice from
Dan Schaeffler

The meeting with Greenway Electronics went well—I'm excited to report that the agreement appears feasible. I went from the airport straight to my office at Autowerke, but I can't help thinking about Heidi. We still haven't had the opportunity to discuss my job offer in depth. We tried a couple of times, but it was just too hard on the phone.

I'm a little hopeful though. In the second call, Heidi had been totally opposed to the move. But in the next call, she was less resolute in her opposition. I could tell because she had already entered problem-solving mode. Her firm does have an office in Fort Wayne—a subsidiary, really more of an affiliate—and there might be an opportunity to transfer. She is also inquiring about how schooling for the kids might work. Maybe everything will work out.

I'm still heavily weighing my options though. Do I really want to do this? I feel guilty about thinking of leaving Autowerke and letting down my long-term mentor, Autowerke's CPO, Dan Schaeffler. I need to talk to Dan—I owe him that after all his help early on at the company. And I know that Dan will not just tell me to stay at Autowerke, but will give me his honest opinion. Still jet-lagged, I head to see Dan.

"Thomas, welcome back! Come in," says Dan as I hover at the door of Dan's office. "Sounds like you had a good week. I see that we are nearly there with the negotiations. Looks like this is going to fly."

"Yes, Dan, it was a good week," I reply, in a less than enthusiastic tone. Dan pauses, scanning my face. I sit down at the table.

"Guess you are tired. You have earned a rest. Why don't you go home early and go spend some time with that lovely wife of yours." I can't make eye contact.

"Dan, I need to talk to you."

"About the deal?" says Dan. "Or ... is something else on your mind?" He gets up and shuts the door.

"Dan, I was offered a job while I was in Chicago."

Dan is a veteran, and very few things seriously faze him these days. It seems this does. "Thomas, I thought you went there to do a deal, not get a new job." But he laughs. "How did this happen?"

"I got talking to the guy next to me on the plane ride over, and it happened to be the CEO of Heartland Consolidated Industries, and one thing kind of led to another. He offered me the CPO role there."

Dan pauses and lets out a deep breath. "That's a pretty big job, Thomas. Heartland also has a reputation for being a hard-nosed organization. Probably more than we are. I met Bailkowsky once. He doesn't take any prisoners."

"He seemed pretty straightforward when we met. But I see your point."

Dan leans back in his chair. "Where would you be based? Fort Wayne? Does Heidi really want to relocate to Indiana, Thomas?"

"It's not her dream location. I'll admit that," I say. "But, I think she would be prepared to make the move for me." I'm still not certain that is true.

"You have a good future here too, Thomas. You are well regarded. The Greenway deal will be another feather in your cap."

"I understand that, Dan," I say in a matter-of-fact tone.

"If you stay, we'd be looking to promote you into a brand CPO role over the next year or so. Or, perhaps a role outside of procurement, if that appealed to you. You might also be able to stay here at Essen. I'm sure we could come to some agreement on location. In other words, your future here is bright."

"That's good of you, Dan, but the Heartland job looks like a real challenge. There seems to be a lot to do there. Their procurement organization is a decade or more behind ours. They need financial results to be delivered, and quickly." I sit back upright. "And I'll be in charge."

"As I said, it's high risk, too. In the top job, you are very much alone. You need to deliver, and there are few people you can trust to give you honest advice. And people who like things the way they are will be gunning for you."

"I realize that. It is a big job. I think I am ready for a new challenge."

"We can give you new challenges here, too," says Dan.

"At Heartland I will be running my own show." I pause and look right into his eyes. "Dan, you have always been honest with me. What would you do in my shoes?"

Dan utters a heavy sigh. Sitting back in his chair again, he looks at the ceiling and then back at me. "In your shoes, I would do it. It is too big of an opportunity to pass up. I'm sure the money he offered you is nice, too. But let me give you some advice first."

"Shoot."

"What you will really need to do well is build a good relationship not just with Ross Bailkowsky but also with the other senior executives. Procurement does not just work in a vacuum where we only negotiate with suppliers. A CPO needs to work well with the rest of the executive team so that they will accept that procurement deserves to have a decision-making role. I think we in procurement here are much further ahead than they are at Heartland Consolidated Industries in being effective internally. I think that will be your biggest personal challenge as CPO. Here, we take internal cooperation for granted. You will miss that at Heartland." Dan stands up and reaches out to shake my hand. "I wish you luck."

CPO Best Practices

- Procurement must have a good relationship with the CEO.

- Procurement must work well with the rest of the executive team.

- A CPO will have to work to convince others that procurement deserves a decision-making role.

Chapter 5:
Working It Out

After meeting with Dan, I take a taxi home—with jet lag, driving seems like a bad idea. As we near home, I ponder Dan's advice. Right now, I think of procurement challenges in relation to how to negotiate externally and manage suppliers. It hadn't occurred to me that internal negotiations in relation to procurement would be a problem. But again, if Heartland's procurement organization is indeed a decade or so behind ours, I might be up against a lot of internal antagonism. People don't like change. Thinking about the implications of this, I can't help but wonder if Dan was trying to dissuade me from accepting the offer. Yet the advice appears honest enough—and it's not Dan's way to hold back ambition.

The kids are excited to see me, and we go through our usual escapades, hearing about the various highlights of their week. The whirlwind of being home and seeing Heidi, who arrived shortly after me, puts Fort Wayne at the center of my thoughts again. I can feel the words that Heidi and I will speak later filling the room around us. I'm exhausted, and Heidi probably wants to wait until we are alone—so we put it off.

It is Saturday morning, so the kids go to their usual morning classes with Ekaterina. I take Heidi to a nearby coffee shop for breakfast.

"So, how was your talk with Dan?" asks Heidi, sipping her coffee.

"He understands why I want to do this," I say.

"It's a big opportunity for you," says Heidi, "I realize that too. But we have a lot of things to work out. Life would be very different."

"I know."

"The children's schooling will be difficult, for a start. David is just coming up to the entrance tests for school and Johanna is in the middle of her second year there. Ideally, we'd need to find a German school for them. I can't find one in Fort Wayne, of course."

"Going to an American school will improve their English, though," I say.

"Ah, but they learn good English here anyway," Heidi replies. "I daresay we will find a way though. They are smart and will excel wherever we are."

"I'm sure they will," I say, feeling a glimmer of hope about the turn the conversation is taking.

"I also need to think about my own job. We do have an affiliate office in Fort Wayne. It's not ideal, I have no clients there, and I'm not a U.S. attorney of course. But there might be a way to make it work with a transfer. I've already started the process. We'll see."

"That's good," I say a little clumsily.

"I'm not sure it will help my long-term career though, Thomas," she says glumly. "It's a distant outpost for our firm. I feel a little like my sister, you do realize. This is putting your career first."

"I know my love," I say in a low tone, "and I love you for it." I don't really know what to say; and the silence from Heidi's end of the table suggests the feeling is mutual. I place my hand over hers, and fill the silence with my own thoughts. The waiter appears out of nowhere, loudly asking if we want anything else. I order a second coffee. I would love something stronger, but 10:00 a.m. is a little early.

As the waiter leaves, Heidi says, "And, of course, all of my friends are here—in Dusseldorf and in Germany. We don't know anyone in Fort Wayne, except those guys you played golf with. I bet everyone golfs there. I've never played, and I've never wanted to either." She giggles, breaking the tension.

"You know, even if I stay at Autowerke, I won't be able to stay at Essen forever. They expect people to move around; not just within Germany, but globally too. Some of the sites are not in very glamorous locations, either. We'd have the same issues. This is just more sudden."

"I understand. But I'll do it. You know, we may even come to like the lifestyle. I mean, there is a lot of space out there in the Midwest. I can only imagine how large our house will be there compared to what we have in Dusseldorf! If we're not careful, we'll spend all our spare time tending the garden. When we're not playing golf that is." Heidi smiles. "I bet it will be more like what we'd call a farm here!"

"I bet it will be—we'll probably be able to play golf in the garden."

"We'll make it work."

I finish my second cup, and we leave the table and walk home arm in arm. Life is going to be very different now.

Interlude

Financial Daily

June 1, 2012

Heartland Consolidated Industries, Inc.—Fort Wayne, Indiana–based food producer Heartland Consolidated Industries has appointed Thomas Sutter as its new Chief Procurement Officer. The procurement manager, with background in the automotive industry, is expected to cut Heartland's costs for external supplies by $1 billion.

Market Journal

June 1, 2012

Heartland to Slash External Expenditures

FORT WAYNE—The global consumer foods giant Heartland Consolidated Industries, Inc., is strengthening its procurement function by creating the position of Chief Procurement Officer at corporate headquarters. The company expects to cut costs of external supplies by $1 billion in the first year.

On Friday, Heartland announced the appointment of Thomas Sutter as its Chief Procurement Officer (CPO), a newly created role reporting directly to the group's CEO, Ross Bailkowsky. Sutter is a high-profile procurement executive from German carmaker Autowerke AG. His company's global procurement initiatives generated multibillion-dollar savings for Autowerke and strengthened the brand's market position through exclusive innovation partnerships with key suppliers. In his new role, Sutter will transfer the procurement expertise he gained in the automotive industry—considered the leading industry in procurement for decades—to Heartland.

Heartland has recently been facing difficult market conditions, including rising commodity prices and increased competition from global food brands, putting its financial results under pressure. Through the stronger centralization of procurement under its new CPO, the company expects major productivity gains. Heartland CEO Bailkowsky says that procurement has been long neglected in the group and that Sutter will deliver savings of at least $1 billion in the first year. Analysts welcomed the announcement, which sent Heartland's stock price up 3.5% on a day the industry sector as a whole dropped 1.6%.

HEART and MIND: The monthly newsletter for the Heartland Consolidated Industries family

July 2012

Procurement shifts gears

An Interview with Thomas Sutter, Our New Chief Procurement Officer

Thomas Sutter joined Heartland Consolidated Industries on June 1 as our new Chief Procurement Officer (CPO), coming from Autowerke AG in Germany. Thomas has just moved with his wife Heidi and his children—a girl (7) and a boy (5)—to Fort Wayne. Let's find out more about Thomas.

HaM: Thomas, first let us welcome you to Heartland. We heard that you arrived in Fort Wayne only few days ago. Have you and your family had any time to get settled yet?

Thomas: Thank you very much for the warm welcome. Well yes, moving the whole family with only a few weeks' advance notice has created some challenges here and there, but we are all extremely excited about the opportunities that Heartland and Fort Wayne are offering us.

HaM: It is quite a change to move from Germany to Indiana. How do you like living in America so far?

Thomas: My father is American—he served in the U.S. Air Force in Germany for many years—so I am familiar with the American way of life. In fact, I have very much been looking forward to the change, in particular to being closer to my parents, who live in Chicago.

HaM: Thomas, you're the first CPO at Heartland. What plans do you have?

Thomas: My mission is to fundamentally change the way procurement is done at Heartland to achieve major savings for the company. In other words, we are here to shift gears now, if you allow me a little bit of automotive jargon.

HaM: Reports say that you have been given a savings target of $1 billion. This is a big number. How are you going to achieve this?

Thomas: Yes, the target is an ambitious one. However, procurement—especially in the automotive industry—has made tremendous advancements over past years. If we introduce their best practices at Heartland, the target will be achievable.

HaM: But building cars is not like feeding millions of people. How can the best practices be transferred between two businesses that are so different?

Thomas: In procurement, the main driver for the strategy is the balance of supply and demand power, and there is a whole arsenal of approaches relating back to that logic. As long as your procurement team is able to handle this, the industry becomes a secondary matter. Buying metal and buying agricultural commodities, for example, will follow similar principles.

HaM: What reaction do you expect from our suppliers? At the end of the day, the savings will have to come from them, right?

Thomas: With more than half of the value added coming externally, going after productivity gains from suppliers is just a reasonable thing to do. And by helping Heartland to increase its competitiveness, our suppliers will sustain their business with us, which is in their very own interest. In fact, we will be working on many "win–win" cases over the next couple of months.

HaM: Thomas, this truly sounds exciting! And now for a little fun—some quick-fire questions to help our readers understand what makes you tick:

Favorite holiday destination:	Iceland; it is in the middle of my two homes—Europe and the United States—and the nature is simply breathtaking.
Most frequented web site:	Apple iTunes
Favorite meal:	Seafood, my Dad's barbecue
Favorite band/singer:	Professor Longhair, a New Orleans legend who is not internationally known but has influenced many famous artists all over the world
Favorite restaurant:	Tokyo Sushi Corner in Dusseldorf, Germany
Favorite sport:	Running and yoga

If you could have any four people over for dinner:

> Abraham Lincoln, Albert Einstein,
> Loriot the German comedian, and
> the Grandpa I never met

Thomas, thank you for your time and allowing us to get to know you a little better. Congratulations on your new role and all the best for the months ahead.

Chapter 6:
Two Disgruntled Heartland Consolidated Industries Procurement Executives

08:12
From: Paul Jackson <pjackson@heartlandconsolidated.com>
To: Gary Parker <gparker@ heartlandconsolidated.com>
Subject: You won't believe it …
Attachments: Heartland to slash external expenditures.pdf (74 KB)

Good morning, Gary,

How was your fishing? Get some nice trout? You won't believe what has happened while you were away …

The good part: Ross seems to finally understand that procurement is important.

The bad: Instead of hiring one of us, he hired a guy from Germany to become CPO! See attachment for the full story. It's so typical … he makes a decision and we learn about it reading the newspaper!

The ugly: I really have no idea how he can think that this guy will be of any help. He's from Autowerke—as if our snacks and cereals are cars or spare parts. And look what savings estimates he is promising—$1b in one year. Is he nuts? Does he really think we have been living behind the Moon?

Gimme a call when you arrive in the office, buddy.

Paul Jackson
Procurement Director
Sweet Grain, a Heartland Consolidated Industries, Inc., company

---

08:55
From: Gary Parker <gparker@ heartlandconsolidated.com>
To: Paul Jackson <pjackson@ heartlandconsolidated.com>
Subject: Re: You won't believe it …

Hi Paul,

Thanks for sending me this … puuh, yeah, quite a surprise. This guy looks like a prig. I'd laugh if it weren't so sad. For years and years we're working our asses off, and then they send us this guy who tells us we are leaving $1b on the table. You know what will happen—as soon as he recognizes that agricultural products are not as easy to source as door handles they will blame everyone else but not themselves. $1b in savings? After all the heat we had in the Midwest? Prices at the Minneapolis Grain Exchange know only one direction now: up!

Will be real funny to see how he wants to do any savings here.

And I guess you remember what I told you about what Ross decided last year and we tried to convince our dear friends from product management to change some recipes.

Good luck, Mr. Gorsky! :-)

Will call you in the afternoon … need to run to a meeting now. Going to see our biggest supplier for yeast.

Gary
Gary Parker
Ingredients Purchasing
Heartland Consolidated Industries, Inc.

09:23
From: Paul Jackson <pjackson@ heartlandconsolidated.com>
To: Gary Parker <gparker@ heartlandconsolidated.com>
Subject: Re: You won't believe it …

Gary,

Maybe we should have some drinks this evening at Joe's. I'll invite Bob and Mitchell. Everyone here is, uh, "surprised."

I just hope that Ross is now finally behind this so that next time our discussions with Marketing or R&D will be a little less painful. Just got another request for a complete new packaging for an N-Bar campaign on my desk. I can be the best negotiator in the world, but as long as they demand small special orders and specs that makes it expensive (6 colors, metallic, lacquering, embossing, extra-thick) …

It's not that we wouldn't have plenty of ideas for generating savings.

BTW, what was this "Mr. Gorsky" thing?

P

12:58
From: Gary Parker <gparker@ heartlandconsolidated.com>
To: Paul Jackson <pjackson@ heartlandconsolidated.com>
Subject: Re: You won't believe it …

Good idea. Let's align and discuss our strategy. Have you heard any timeline about when he is going to arrive? Heard rumors about next Monday but nothing confirmed yet.

The meeting with our yeast supplier was, as expected, "interesting." Of course he had seen the article and was asking me what would change now, as if I know. But the good thing: he was offering to increase our discount from 2 to 3% if we would agree on a 5y contract. Nice.

On a completely different note, I remember you presented a little while ago an "e-auction" tool. Are you guys still using it? Was thinking about giving it a try on some of the barley we need for our plant in Kentucky.

Gorsky—I was remembering that story about what Neil Armstrong supposedly said when he landed on the Moon. Only an urban legend, but a funny one. Just Google "Good luck, Mr. Gorsky."
Gary

Gary Parker
Ingredients Purchasing
Heartland Consolidated Industries, Inc.

2:03
From: Paul Jackson <pjackson@ heartlandconsolidated.com>
To: Gary Parker <gparker@ heartlandconsolidated.com>
CC: Robert Michalsky <rmichalsky@h heartlandconsolidated.com>
Subject: Re: You won't believe it …

☺ Man that was funny.

About the e-Auction tool you should contact Bob (copied here). Honestly, I haven't worked much with it. We had some technical difficulties and very little training. Maybe we are finally getting approval for a better and integrated e-Procurement and e-Sourcing solution? Don't know exactly what we need but I do know what we currently have is crap.

See you at 7 at Joe's.

P

Chapter 7:
Have We Done
the Right Thing?

I open my eyes Saturday morning to an awful day—wind and rain. Johanna and David are playing video games.

Heidi comes in and once she sees I'm awake, says, "Hear that? I would reprimand them if I knew what they could be doing somewhere else. Coffee will be ready in a minute," she adds.

I gaze about the room. Boxes and packing crates are everywhere, just waiting for Heidi and me to unpack them. I look out the window, waiting for the coffeemaker to finish—it was one of the first things we unpacked. Heidi sits down on the bed.

"We still have so much to unpack," she says. "This will take forever. I've never liked moving."

"Yes it is a chore," I say.

"What do people do on weekends in a town like this," she asks. "Do you think there are even coffee shops? You can't even play golf in this weather."

"Of course there are coffee shops," I say. "I passed a nice mall on my way to the office yesterday, and multiple Starbucks."

"Pssh. You know Starbucks isn't what I mean. We don't even know anyone to go to a coffee shop with. Except ourselves."

"I know. But we will get to know people," I say. "People here are friendly. Look, we've already had two of our neighbors come to welcome us—both of them bringing food. You wouldn't get that in Germany, now, would you? I thought that was very nice."

"They are friendly, but we don't really know anyone, properly, that is. And, I'm not really sure what to talk to people about," she says. "I don't feel like I have a great deal in common with anyone, and I'm nervous about my own English. I'm also worrying about the children settling into school. It starts in six weeks. The curriculum is so different, and having to take all of their classes in English will be difficult for them. I think we will have to hire a tutor to help get them up to speed in English."

"They play soccer here—that's what Americans call football. That will be great for David."

"Yes, they do play 'soccer,' " she says, practicing the word. "But, that's not the only criterion, is it?"

"I know it's not, but it's a start. We have to start somewhere. How was the office yesterday?"

"Oh, it was fine," she says. "Different from Dusseldorf, but similar work really. I think that it will be all right. I can't really be licensed here unless I take the bar exam, but I can do some international work for our clients as well as others who need advice on law in Germany or Europe. How was Heartland, by the way? Sounded like things were not that wonderful from what you said last night."

"Hard to tell. I'm not sure if this is just what I should be expecting anyway, or whether it is something more fundamental."

"Like what? Tell me."

"Well, Ross has announced some pretty big targets, of course. You saw the comments in the *Market Journal*. Not everyone is happy about him ignoring the procurement guys and making me CPO. I think people feel threatened, and most of the procurement people at Heartland are lifers. I'm an outsider to them. I think they see me as Ross's guy. They're bound to think that. They're also worried. It's not an easy situation. There's already tension when I enter a room. I'm not convinced everyone is giving me honest answers to questions, either. Some of that I expect I guess, but it feels worse. Seems they also feel they can pull the wool over the eyes of the automotive guy."

"You might just be imagining things," she says. "It's only been two days. Bit early to jump to conclusions."

"I hope so," I say. "But, a few things worry me. Yesterday, I asked if anybody has category and supplier strategies. You know the type of thing—the three-year plans that I am used to seeing at Autowerke. These always included a clear view of the supply-and-demand drivers for the category and a clear articulation of our plans for negotiations, competitive sourcing, demand management, and specification change. None of this seems to be there."

"Thomas, I'm a lawyer, not a procurement person. That doesn't mean much to me."

"Yes, but you can see the point. There are no plans. Everyone is fighting fires. Maybe I just haven't cracked the code they work by yet, but it all seems really unstructured. I'm also not clear that the procurement people work well with the other groups. At Autowerke, we prided ourselves on how well we did that. We even sat together—the marketing category head within the procurement function sat next door to the marketing vice president, for example. At Heartland, the procurement people are all in their own office. They seem to stay there all day, too. And I haven't seen too many suppliers around the last couple of days either. They don't have enough meeting rooms to see suppliers in anyway. None of this on its own is a major finding. But putting it all together suggests that something is seriously wrong. I think they are all spending their time much more on administration than on driving things. I can see why Ross is not happy with how things are right now."

Heidi smiles and says, "Well, Mr. Hotshot CPO, he didn't bring you all the way from Dusseldorf because he was happy, did he?"

"No, he didn't," replies Thomas. "But, things feel a lot more backward than I expected. Dan did warn me of this. Perhaps I should have listened to him. What I do know is that achieving $1 billion will be difficult, maybe even impossible, in the current setup. That is clear."

"You're not having regrets, are you, Thomas Sutter—after dragging the three of us halfway around the world?"

I can hear the sarcasm in her voice. "No, no regrets. I like a challenge," I say. But she can tell I'm not 100% sure of my answer. As I cut open a box, I wonder if we made the right decision.

| CPO Best Practices |

- Effective procurement requires internal relationships to be managed, as well as external ones.

- Procurement needs to drive a strategic agenda, with category strategies in place for all major spend areas.

- Procurement needs to deploy the bulk of its resources for value-creating strategic work; internal administration should be reduced, simplified, and automated.

Chapter 8:
A Day in Thomas's Life at Heartland Consolidated Industries

I had to leave earlier in the morning from home – before the kids got up

So I went into the meetings, which took longer than expected.

Sorry, can you join a negotiation?

My team waits until they are almost done with negotiations before inviting me to the meeting.

I've now been on the job for more than a month. I am two hours late leaving Heartland. I missed David's summer league soccer game. It's so much fun watching six-year-olds chasing the ball in a pack. I'm sure he's disappointed that I'm not there. Heidi will be too—she thinks I don't spend enough time with the kids. I would love to spend more time with them. It's just not possible right now.

Today I had to leave the house earlier than usual—before the kids even got up—because I had two internal meetings with logistics and production. There are multiple problems there, and procurement is accused of being their cause. Both meetings took longer than expected, making my morning quite lengthy. They scoffed at me, asking how I could provide "the $1 billion in savings when we cannot even source a logistics provider efficiently?" I wasn't even appointed CPO yet when the logistics request and supplier selection took place. The meetings went on so long that I had to change my appointment time with a supplier to find some new, ad hoc logistic forwarders. I ran to the supplier meeting, which had started without me, and everything was already set before the negotiation between engineering and the supplier started. My category leader was barely able to negotiate terms and conditions.

I'm also starving right now, because I had to skip lunch. Of course, I ended up making an unhealthy choice and eat a chocolate bar instead. This has been happening a lot lately. When I feel miserable in the way things are going, I tend to eat junk food. This is why I normally plan a fixed half hour for lunch. Just before I wanted to go to lunch today, though, I was asked by Tom Blissoe— category leader for oils—to join a negotiation. This is a major sourcing group within Heartland, and I asked my team to inform me if negotiations are going on with the supplier from whom we buy more than $500,000 of product. Blissoe had not informed me about anything untoward in his sourcing group. When I entered the room, I knew why he asked me to join. The supplier wanted a price increase of 15% and said that he could also sell his oils to other companies. I interrupted the negotiation and played a risky card, saying we would not accept any increases at the moment.

I asked Tom to step aside with me right away and asked for his negotiation strategy. He answered that there was no strategy. Normally, the supplier asks for something, then Heartland counters, and they end somewhere in the middle. I'm shocked. No strategy, no tactics. I asked him about alternatives to this specific supplier. He mentioned that there are not really alternatives on the market. Heartland has worked with this supplier for decades, and the product managers would not accept any other supplier for oils. Astonished, I told Tom to spend the next week looking for other supplier options, and then let me know what he finds. He seemed to sneer in accepting the order and let me know that I'd probably messed up a good thing with the oil vendor.

I have observed similar things numerous times these past couple of days. My team waits until they are almost done with negotiations before inviting me to the meeting, and then I am there to chair final negotiations with suppliers who are asking for increases in cost. But when there are price decreases I am not invited. The team appears to want to take the full credit for these. I know I am being manipulated by my own team. It does not really seem fair to me, but I know it's happening.

By the time the meeting with our oil supplier ended, I was very behind in my agenda for the day. When I have to postpone all my meetings with colleagues by one or two hours, pushing delays back for the entire day, it creates a bad impression. I feel like I have to do firefighting all day and can't focus on strategic work. Speaking with my team even underlines this impression—they all work on transactions. When I request some strategic work, they claim they don't have time for it and lack resources, and that that is done by other departments anyway. Honestly, my impact here as CPO is far less than it was in Autowerke as a category leader.

CPO Best Practices

- Effective negotiations require a clear strategy and a good understanding of the alternatives, and these are prepared in advance.

- Procurement and internal customers/stakeholders need to be jointly involved in the sourcing process from early on to agree on requirements, set specifications, and explore alternative options.

- Procurement needs to challenge and change entrenched business views that overly restrict the available supplier and specification options.

Chapter 9:
In Ross's Office

Getting a slot in Ross's calendar is difficult. He's traveling a good 70% of the time and when he is in his office, just about everyone wants or needs to meet with him. Looking back, it seems the longest conversation I've had with Ross was on our flight from Frankfurt to Chicago. "Maybe I should take more long-haul flights with Ross," I mutter to myself. I pick up the phone and dial Helen, Ross's assistant.

Helen is the epitome of Midwestern cheerfulness. "Thomas, sorry to keep you waiting for so long. Ross just bumped Kevin Borr off his calendar when he heard that you wanted to meet with him. Can you come over in 30 minutes?" I'm happy that despite the many frustrations I've had with my own team, Ross still has me high on his list of priorities. I collect my things and take the short stroll over to the his office.

Apart from the telephone and the computer screens, Ross's office looks like something out of the 1920s. Dark-paneled walls complement the heavy leather furniture. Not my style, but somehow very much in tune with Ross. Seeing me enter, Ross immediately gets up from behind his desk and ushers me to sit down in one of the heavy sofas. Helen walks in to serve us tea and coffee together with the brand of low-fat cookies Heartland has recently launched.

"In the past twelve months, we have sold one billion of these," Ross says. "Think about it, every American from baby to retiree has had three of these. So tell me, how is business? Have you settled in already?"

"Things are just fine," I lie. "I am here to get your green light for launching a formal cost-down initiative."

"That's exactly what I hired you for, Thomas. What exactly do you mean by a 'formal' initiative, though?"

I explained what I had in mind. We would systematically look at every single spend category across the business from oils and flavors to packaging and IT (information technology). For each one, we would assess the current balance of demand and supply power and identify the appropriate approaches. These would range from forcing greater competition—which I instinctively felt was needed in oils, especially—through to specification change, demand reduction, and more intensive supplier collaboration. We would then compare this with what Heartland was already doing. I was confident that in nearly all cases, Heartland was not doing the best it could do in these categories. The gap between what we should be doing and what we were doing would enable us to set category-level savings targets and really drive cost reduction on a strategic and systematic basis.

We would drive the work by setting up empowered category teams. In a first for Heartland—although a commonplace at Autowerke—these would be multidisciplinary. They would include specialists from procurement but also finance, marketing, IT, and research and development. The precise team mix would vary with the actual category needs.

Ross listened without interrupting, only nodding in agreement with my key points.

"Well this is what I call a coincidence," he says once I'm finished. "I had actually wanted to see you to discuss something very similar."

Ross explained the challenges Heartland Consolidated Industries is facing. They have become the focus of a host of pressure groups accusing them of being one of the main reasons there is such a high obesity rate in America. Some school districts are planning on banning Heartland's products altogether, and there is a YouTube hit with several mock commercials for "Heartdisease" products. Heartland is taking these accusations very seriously and has developed new, healthier products at an astonishingly fast rate. These investments, along with falling sales of more traditional products, have taken a heavy toll on Heartland's profitability.

Under pressure from the stock market, Ross has decided to launch a comprehensive cost-cutting program addressing all areas of Heartland. He wants me to be the spearhead of this program by delivering significant, and fast, savings in procurement. He expects me to do this Autowerke style, taking all the divisions and business units with me.

"Thomas, you are the one to pave the way for the other functions. All our senior people here in global headquarters are Americans. They can be effective here, but will they be effective in Europe and Asia? You are different in being both American and European. Show the others how to do it." Before I could think to say anything, or ask myself whether I was hired for my procurement experience or my multicultural upbringing, the meeting was over. "Think about what you want me to do to make this one a success," Ross says as I head for the door.

On my way back, I attempt to digest what just happened. On the upside I have the green light for my procurement initiative. Also, I'm getting a lot of visibility, probably more visibility than I want at the moment. On the downside, the way Ross has explained the program, this would mean that I will have to spend a lot of time in Europe and even Asia. How will Heidi react to this? I make her and the kids move from Dusseldorf to Fort Wayne only to have to go and do projects in Europe! Heidi is not going to be a fan of this.

CPO Best Practices

- Top-down sponsorship is crucial for strategic procurement initiatives to work effectively.

- An understanding of demand and supply power in categories is crucial for identifying untapped opportunities.

- Cross-functional category teams are essential for delivering results.

Chapter 10: Unhappiness Everywhere

I can't believe it! The head of production and one of our key contractors for supplying and installing machinery are collaborating with one another? And they are collaborating with one another against procurement and against me? How did this happen?

I can't believe it! The head of production and one of our key contractors for supplying and installing machinery are collaborating with one another? And they are collaborating with one another against procurement and against me? How did this happen? In my naivety, I assumed that the head of production and head of procurement would fight together to achieve benefits for Heartland Consolidated Industries. How silly of me. I knew there was a problem in internal communication. It seems we are in the process of investing heavily in a new processing plant—a major CAPEX [capital expenditure] project for us. When I reviewed it, comparing some investments to those we did at Autowerke, I saw that the price was much too high. Now I know that we can't completely compare a car plant with a food processing plant, but based on previous experiences, I have developed a skill in feeling out price levels. Additionally, the second-ranked supplier is offering a similar processing plant solution for 75% of the price! Amazing!

Rick Fiore, the head of production, explained to me that we can't change suppliers. Heartland has been using the same one for decades, it knows Heartland's processes, and it is close to the work site.

I realize that I didn't even get a notice or invitation for the planning meetings for this new investment—it was literally news to me.

Here's how it unfolded: Ross stopped by and asked me if I was excited about the new processing plant, which would probably be the most valuable contract this year. I stood there like a bumbling idiot and admitted that I had no clue what he was talking about.

I called Rick right away; as per usual he did not answer his cell—and he never calls back either—so I walked to his office directly. I knocked on his door and asked about the investment. I'm surprised by how enthusiastic he was about it, even offering me a cup of coffee.

Rick pulled out some drawings and explained the new plan to me: the quantity, the technical innovations this processing plant represented, the huge increases in productivity at Heartland, and finally the price—a multimillion-dollar processing plant with the highest possible specifications anybody could imagine. When he got to the price, I questioned him as to why I was not involved. At this, Rick started laughing.

Condescendingly, he stated, "Thomas, this is a rather complex processing plant—not copy paper or simple products. This is engineering—so honestly, there is nothing for procurement to do. I negotiated everything with the supplier already and this is really the best price for this configuration. And as always I will leave 3% for procurement success, so that you can negotiate and book a win."

So apparently I am part of the meetings going forward, but any questions I ask are not answered or basically ignored. There was also a peculiar incident: one of the young potentials—the engineer in charge of this plant, who works for Rick and was in his office at the time—came up to me later and said that

I asked the right questions. The suppliers on the short list were interchangeable, and in some performance metrics, the current number two was even better.

I knew this was the best argument for having procurement being more involved in negotiations. As well as the backing from Ross, I gathered all the material and quotes I needed to prepare for the negotiation with Rick. However, it seems Rick and I can't work together—he is reluctant to align with a negotiation strategy, threatening the supplier with loss of business and welcoming new suppliers.

What a contrast. I remember clearly how Frank Kaufmann at Autowerke— the engineering procurement leader—and myself would spend nights preparing a negotiation strategy and finally achieving really great results. We sometimes changed suppliers that had worked for Autowerke for years—and not only to achieve good savings, but to have competition around, and to have access to new developments. When Frank was thinking about new ideas, he always asked me first, describing his idea, asking for my opinion and for support on the supplier market. We screened the market for ideas and solutions. One of the key success factors was that we worked so closely together and had a clear strategy when working the supplier market.

Maybe Dad was right. I don't know what I'm getting into. Is this just the United States? Is this the industry? Is this Heartland? Is it a different understanding of procurement in general? I have to admit this is the first time I've been quite unhappy and doubting my decision. What happens if I fail here?

When it rains it pours: Heidi is quite unhappy here as well. She just texted complaining about another facet of Fort Wayne. She was nearly hit by a truck when she was running. There aren't even sidewalks here to go running on. In general, she thinks that there is nothing really to do here, no social life, nothing—and I have to admit, she is right. I don't care as much as she does, since I work and travel a lot. Honestly, I am quite happy just coming home and doing nothing on the weekends, maybe just having some barbecue with the kids. And Heidi does like that a lot. We just bought a Weber gas grill—I love it. I feel that on one hand we are very close as a family, but on the other hand we are very isolated. The kids are pretty integrated at school—although not as much as in Germany. It is most difficult for Heidi. She sees herself as a victim of my career. This makes me sad as well. I know I am partially responsible for this.

Things are getting worse. We just had our negotiation with the processing plant contractor.

The situation between Rick and me collapsed in the negotiation with "his" supplier. I questioned the basis of the proposal, showing some analysis and cost comparisons. The supplier smiled at me and said, "You can easily switch to another supplier, who is probably cheaper. But if you switch and I have to divert resources that are currently dedicated to Heartland for several plant upgrades to other projects, you will have to live with the consequences."

Rick was immediately concerned and tried to calm down the supplier with the words I will not forget: "No, no. We need you and we will not put you under so much pressure. We know what you have done for Heartland Consolidated Industries over the years and we really honor this relationship. You probably are a bit more expensive, but we know that this is because of the quality and that you always meet the timeframes agreed on." The supplier smiled as if he were in complete control. Which apparently he was, at least in Rick's view. Unbelievable. The most embarrassing thing was when he said, "Sorry, but Thomas is from procurement and quite new in the company. He does not know our culture here."

I attempted to stay calm, taking some deep breaths, and I made several new attempts to negotiate. But I failed. The alliance—production and supplier—is too strong. After the meeting, Rick shouted at me in front of several colleagues, saying that I was risking the success of Heartland, and that my attitude and behavior is "unacceptable." If the production volume of products with large contributions to margin are delayed this season, they can't be made up later. Rick left and I could tell he was heading to Ross's office to complain. I don't know what went on in that office, but Ross has told me I have to come to terms with Rick.

CPO Best Practices

- Procurement needs to manage stakeholder relationships systematically, and gain acceptance to act as a business partner.

- Procurement must get involved in evaluating the options for sourcing needs early on.

- Before walking into a negotiation, the team must be fully aligned on the strategy and needs to have rehearsed messages—and act as a team with production and others.

Interlude

America Today
September 23, 2012
HEART(land) DISEASE
Opinion: Finally Time for a Diet?

FORT WAYNE—Everybody hails growth, but no one asks whether this is healthy. The convenience food industry—or food giant Heartland Consolidated Industries, to give it a name and a face—has been growing tremendously over the past years. And it has been making billions and billions of dollars in profit. But who pays the bill in the end? In fact, we do. And we do it twice: First for the junk food and then for the cure.

Happily paying premium prices for carbs plus 35% fat in yummy products like "real tasty French Frites," or for candies made of almost pure sugar (called "HeartLabama's Sweeties" for better marketing), America's population is growing, too. *We* are growing. But … we are getting bigger literally. In the last few years, we have witnessed an incredible surge in obesity rates in our country, along with all the typical health problems. They range from Aunt Annie's aching joints to Uncle Herman's heart attack (why did it happen when he was still so young?).

However, something's cooking now: Heartland's sales have stagnated recently, and have even started to drop, along with its profits. Is it because America is getting smarter? Is it because *we* are finally getting smarter? Indeed, there is now an increasing demand for healthy food. Consumption patterns are beginning to change for the better—the health food market is picking up. Finally, the time seems to have come for a diet—for us and for the Heartlands in this world. It's in our hands!

Financial Daily
Friday 10/02/2012
STOCKS AT BOTTOM

Heartland Consolidated Industries Stock Downgraded to "Sell."
Food producer Heartland has posted disappointing third-quarter results, with sales down by 6% and profits slashed by 75% compared to the third quarter in 2011. The company did not give an outlook for the end of the year or 2013. With its conservative product portfolio, Heartland seems less prepared to weather the continued economic weakness than its competitors, who have entered into the health food segment where sales are increasing against

market trends with stable margins. Despite a planned program to reduce procurement costs by $5 billion, Heartland is in a clear "sell" position.

Market Journal
October 2, 2012
Heartland Stroke By Recession

FORT WAYNE—Food giant Heartland Consolidated Industries, Inc., has posted the weakest third quarter (Q3) numbers in its history. While the company remains profitable—barely—it blames a weak economy and sluggish demand for domestic consumer products for the disappointing results. It announced an unprecedented cost-cutting program.

Yesterday, Heartland announced its results for the Q3 of 2012. With sales down by 6% to $15.3 billion from $16.3 billion in Q3 2011 and profit by 75% to $490 million from $1.95 billion, the company has posted its largest profit decline in four decades. The full-year results will look more stable due to a strong first quarter—assuming the food giant gets back on track in the current quarter. In light of the potential for a genuine recession, however, Heartland's management refused to give an outlook for the end of the year or 2013. Instead, an ambitious cost-reduction program was announced by Heartland CEO Ross Bailkowsky in a letter to shareholders.

"In the current market, tackling external spend is our most effective productivity lever," Bailkowsky writes. "Therefore, Heartland is about to launch a firm-wide procurement program worth $5 billion in savings. The program will be headed by our CPO. With the first savings hitting the bottom line in the first quarter, we expect a quick rebound of Heartland's financial performance."

Few analysts share Bailkowsky's optimism, however. Many see Heartland's decision not to enter the growing health food market as one of the main reasons for the disappointing results. Most have downgraded Heartland stock to "sell." On Wall Street, Heartland stock prices were down 7.1% yesterday.

Chapter 11:
Humiliated

I ran for an hour, and felt much better. During the run, my mind turned away from Rick to my big day tomorrow, when I will be launching the $5 billion initiative to the global procurement team.

Increasingly cheerful, I took the turn back to home.

At dinner, Heidi asks me about my big day tomorrow and for a minute it's almost like being back in Dusseld

After dinner, I retreat to my study to prepare for my meeting.

One of my mantras is to never let people or circumstances keep me from pursuing my goals. This has served me well in the past when facing professional challenges. I usually go running to relieve the stress and anger of a particularly difficult day. So after the blowup with Rick, I went home and put my running clothes on. Since Heidi's close encounter with that truck, we have limited our running to neighborhoods and the city center, especially where they have sidewalks. Because it is dark outside after work, I would not have run out by the cornfields anyway. I ran for an hour, and felt much better—calmer even. During the run, my mind turned away from Rick to my big day tomorrow, when I will be launching the $5 billion initiative to the global procurement team. I am hopeful that the team will get behind the goal and that we can work together to make it happen. Things are never as bad as they seem at first glance.

I have been at Heartland for less than five months. I could easily attribute what went wrong to an adjustment period. But as my own harshest critic, I will not do that. So far, maybe people haven't noticed that I consider this a glancing blow. Besides, on my run I put together a great plan for meeting that $5 billion target. It will incorporate everything I learned at Autowerke. I will analyze Heartland's total spend—to immediately identify the quick wins—and then pull together category teams to systematically develop strategies to reduce supplier costs. This is just the beginning, but already I feel better. The run was definitely time well spent.

I decide not to tell Heidi about Rick Fiore since she's tired of hearing me complain. We chat while preparing dinner. Heidi asks me about my big day tomorrow, and for a minute it's almost like being back in Dusseldorf. After dinner, I retreat to my study to prepare for my meeting. An upside to living in Fort Wayne is the size of our house. In Dusseldorf, my desk was in our bedroom—so if Heidi went to bed before me, I had to take my laptop somewhere else. Now we both have our own studies. Mine looks out over the backyard and the cornfield. I put some Professor Longhair into the stereo and flip through the PowerPoint deck. The organization of my music database is very reassuring.

Beep. Beep. Beep. I hit the alarm clock. Waking up at 5 is a difficult habit to get used to, but Heartland tends to have big meetings with overseas participants at 7, so I roll out of bed. I turn on the coffeemaker, glance at my iPhone to check my e-mails, and freeze. The purchasing director of our biggest business unit in North America—conveniently based in Fort Wayne—won't make it to the meeting because of "severe operational issues in one of the recently upgraded plants." He will be sending his deputy. The purchasing director of the meat products plant was stuck at the Dallas airport overnight because of heavy rain. So two of the three key North American purchasing directors won't be at the meeting. I don't buy it. This wouldn't have happened at Autowerke. There, the deputy would fix the operational issues and people would find alternatives rather than get stuck at airports. I can feel my anger bubbling up.

I am in the meeting room at six o'clock to double check everything. The coffee, tea, muffins, bagels with cream cheese, are all here. The projector is working, and I have plenty of copies of my slide deck. I personally arrange the seating to avoid crowding and to allow the 40 participants to mingle. Of the 40 invited participants, I only know the North American contingent and seven out of the 17 Europeans.

By 7:00 a.m., there are 30 people in the room—among them six Americans (one is the deputy), the purchasing director of the joint Japanese operations, and 15 Europeans. Among the Europeans is a somewhat annoying Austrian who was clearly excited about his first trip to the United States, and whose English is barely comprehensible. What he lacks in language skills he compensates for in volume. I decide to make a point and start the meeting without waiting for latecomers.

The self-introductions are useful, and I make an effort to memorize all the faces of the people I don't know. After presenting the overall cost reduction program and the specific procurement portion, I ask participants how they feel about the $5 billion objective. There is silence. I pick the deputy purchasing director of the largest business unit. And I ask again. His response is a long lament about increasing wheat prices, production breakdowns, shortages in packaging, and the unreasonable demands marketing was making. As if prompted, several others chime in with similar hard-luck stories. I can barely manage to end it by announcing a coffee break.

After the break, I continue to lay out my plan. Normally I am a very engaging presenter, comfortable with all sorts of audiences. But today is the first time I am presenting to a stone-cold audience. Every face in the room is blank. No one laughs at my well-timed jokes, except the Austrian, and I can feel beads of sweat on my forehead and my voice getting coarse. Before completely losing it, I manage to send everyone to a breakout session on how to collect data for spend analysis. The results of the breakout are disheartening. People can be very creative about why certain things won't work, and what type of IT investments will be required before anything can happen.

The meeting drags on like this until it finally ends at noon. I am exhausted, not to mention downbeat. I stop by my office to drop off my stuff and head out to another meeting across town. On the way to the parking lot I run into Rick, who smirks and says, "I heard today's meeting went really well."

| CPO Best Practices |

- To really make a change initiative succeed, you need to "connect" at the emotional level with the team and not just focus on content.

- To build the necessary support requires considerable behind-the-scenes engagement with the team—a formal presentation, however slick, will not be enough.

- Never underestimate how much energy needs to be devoted to building the team and managing the people as individuals.

Chapter 12:
Enter John McGrath

Driving is still something that helps me gather my thoughts. So rather than fly to Chicago for a barbecue at my parent's house, I decide to drive. I halfheartedly ask Heidi if she wants to ride along, but she declines, saying that she needs a day off. My parents visited us a month ago, so they won't be miffed.

It's Saturday, and I am relieved to be free from pressure both at work and at home. I'm grateful for the way dad and I can communicate. Not a man of many words, he is fine if he doesn't hear from me for weeks at a time, because he figures everything is okay. But I know that I can always turn to him for advice, which I need after the humiliating experience at the procurement directors meeting. I can't talk to Heidi about it, since she is really stressed out about her job. She probably would blame me for rushing into an adventure without considering the consequences, and, I'm beginning to think, rightfully so.

My father immediately recognizes the dire state of affairs. "Hey, this does not sound like anything we can deal with over the phone," he said. "Why don't you come over tomorrow afternoon? We are throwing a barbecue for some friends. It might be one of the last warm days of the year. Do you remember John McGrath? He will be there." I only have a vague memory of John. He's an old friend of my father's. They served in Vietnam together, and when he came around, he always brought model airplane and rocket kits for me.

When I pull into the driveway, I can already smell the barbecue. Three cars are parked on the curb. My mother meets me at the door: "Pass auf, mach dich nicht schmutzig," she says—Careful, don't get yourself dirty—and I give her a hug. She has just finished preparing the burgers and the toppings in the kitchen. I admire that her German still doesn't have the slightest hint of an American accent despite living in an almost exclusively English-speaking environment for so many years.

The afternoon is mostly uneventful. My parent's friends are pleasant. I pull out my wallet to show pictures and get compliments for my beautiful wife and children. By sunset, all of the guests have left except John. The four of us clean up the leftovers and dishes and then sit on the porch enjoying the bottle of Riesling I brought. "So tell us what's going on," my father encourages.

I start recounting the events of the past few weeks. None of the tricks that I had applied so successfully at Autowerke seem to work at Heartland. Everyone there but Ross Bailkowsky seems to despise me. It's just a matter of time before it will become apparent that I've utterly failed and then there is no way back to Autowerke. To make things worse, I've brought Heidi into an impossible situation and now I'm all but risking my marriage by deserting her in Fort Wayne to work on a helpless cause.

Despite my usually upbeat and optimistic nature, it feels good to indulge in a bit of self-pity. My parents and John listen quietly. Finally, my father speaks. "You know son, life has taught me some lessons. One very important one is that it is never as bad or as good as it seems at first glance. So relax, give your best, and you will see that it will be fine in the end."

I want to say that maybe my best isn't good enough, but it doesn't seem appropriate. So I say nothing. Maybe it was stupid of me to run to my father for advice. That's something you do when you're a kid, not when you're a grown man.

My father turns to John. "What's your take on this?" John draws on his pipe and slowly exhales the smoke.

"Well, I don't know anything about procurement. But I do know something about dealing with people. Seems like you have some hefty people issues at hand."

"Thomas, I have never told you, but John here is one of our nation's unsung heroes. After the war, he served as a diplomat, and without him we could have fought several more wars the size of Vietnam. So, I recommend that you listen to him."

Before I can say anything, John stands up: "Happy to talk Thomas, but not tonight. I need my sleep. Meet me at my boat tomorrow morning for breakfast. Your father knows where to find it." With this, he says goodbye, kisses Mom on the cheek, and heads to his car.

Chapter 13:
Capture the Hearts and
Minds of the People

I arrive at the harbor, park the car, and head for John's boat.

It is a beautiful morning, clear sky, no clouds, and some wind.
John is below decks making bacon and eggs, and the smell
wafts up from inside the boat.

As always, he does not say anything in the beginning.

Yes – it's a great place.

It's really great out here. Has to be really nice to own such a boat and spend time here.

Then he begins talking, saying he was surprised last night when I started talking about my problems at work so openly.

If you really want a transformation Thomas, you have to first capture the hearts and minds of people.

We spend the whole day on the water, just sailing, enjoying nature.

I'm anxious to see John again. It was nice to get everything out in the open last night. Hopefully, he doesn't think I'm a complainer. When I first started at Autowerke, people said I complained too much. I think I've changed a lot since then, but sometimes negative thoughts creep back in.

I arrive at the harbor, park the car, and head for John's boat. It's a restored wooden yacht—I suppose 80 or 90 years old. Later, John tells me that the boat is 98 years old and has been in his family since it was first built. It is a beautiful morning, clear sky, no clouds, and some wind. The wind isn't strong, but enough to go sailing. John is below deck making bacon and eggs, and the smell wafts up from inside the boat. I brought some fresh bread and yogurt. On the table near the cockpit is a large bowl of fruit. I sit down and we have breakfast. He doesn't say anything in the beginning. I attempt to start a conversation: "It's really great out here. Has to be really nice to own such a boat and spend time here."

"Yes, it's a great place," he says.

So how can I learn from this man who doesn't talk? Next try: "The pineapple tastes great, really ripe. Back in Germany we had so many hard pineapples."

John says, "Fruit needs time to ripen." Just when I think the conversation has again stalled he continues. "Fruit is the most important thing in the morning for me. It's like tasting nature, life, and feels like I am doing something valuable for my health. It's really important to be fit. This does not mean that you have to run a marathon, but to be physically fit and have some mental dexterity."

Then he begins talking, saying he was surprised last night when I started talking about my problems at work so openly. He said he thought about it a lot last night and again on his way to the boat today. He got to the boat at six o'clock this morning, he said, because he loves to see the sunrise from the boat.

"Thomas—we are sitting here on my boat and I've already seen a very nice sunrise. I love it, when the sun comes up and switches night into day, dark into light, and cold into warm weather. For me, the sunrise represents newness, which attracts a lot of people. It goes to our feelings. You've probably experienced it yourself."

Honestly, for me, this is all quite deep and a bit too much psychology this early in the morning. But he is right. Though admittedly I've never thought about the sunrise like this.

"And," he continues, "this is part of the answer to your problem at Heartland. You are too focused on milestones, meetings, and schedules. These are all very important, but they are not enough. Do you ever think about the feelings of your people, how you can gain their trust, how you can get them to be passionate in their jobs,? How doing that makes *you* more successful?" He then starts to tell me a story about how he managed to help topple a dictator in South America without funding and without any bloodshed. I recall that he was officially in the diplomatic corps, but that my father once said, "He's probably CIA."

He talks about the revolution in Nueva Andalucía, admitting that he took part in it. I'm sitting here on a boat with a man who changed the future of an entire Latin American country. "I got the order from the President himself to 'see what I could do' to encourage a dictator, who was looting his country and killing his own citizens, to give up power—and all without connecting the United States to the outcome. To me, it was clear that this major change after more than 35 years of dictatorship had to happen from within. People have to be passionate to bring about something new. This is why my team and I went to Nueva Andalucía.

On the ground, we tried to understand the mood of the people, their beliefs, and the political system. We identified two issues to address—isolation and malnutrition—and developed a plan. We agreed that the United States would offer food support, which we knew from past experience the Nueva Andalucían government would decline. In the southeast of the country, we had close ties with universities and the creative communities. Once the government declined our offer, the "intelligencia" started demonstrating, and we managed to start a media campaign with local support. As the Nueva Andalucían army stormed the press rooms and began to turn on the students and professors, it was broadcast on television. Citizens, hungry and tired, could not believe their government had refused an offer from the United States to send food. That night, hundreds of thousands of people were in the streets demonstrating against their government. The numbers grew. By the third day, the dictator resigned without a fight. Behind the scenes, we had arranged a backup plan for him to leave the country. So a bloodless revolution took place because we had won the hearts and minds of the people."

John pauses, then continues. "If you really want a transformation, Thomas, you have to first capture the hearts and minds of people. It's not always easy to do, as you can see in my case. But if you have an overall plan and the right message, you will be successful." A seagull flies by us and picks up some bread that fell on the boat deck during breakfast. I'm thinking about his words when John goes down into the cabin to refill our coffee cups. He hoists the sails and we leave the small marina and head out to the open water. There is enough wind for us to travel around 5 knots. I love the wind against my face.

He doesn't speak again, so I try to speak, "About that—," when he interrupts me.

"Thomas, you did a lot of complaining last night. Honestly, do you feel that you are often a victim at Heartland—a victim of your colleagues?"

Well, I think, yes.

He looks at me, standing at the helm. "I'm responsible for the boat. I can decide what to do. I can't blame the wind, the lake, or anybody else for anything that happens. I'm the author. I write the script. And this is exactly what you have to do in your life and how you need to change. You currently feel like a victim."

Ouch. I'm not used to people speaking so plainly. But he doesn't slow down.

"Take a specific event or stimulus. If a victim has a direct negative feeling as an inner reaction, the external reaction will be negative as well. For example, you meet a friend and he is late. As a victim, your inner reaction is that you're upset. When your friend comes, your external reaction will be negative and you will not have a nice evening together. As a more conscious author of your experiences, you wouldn't have an immediate negative reaction if he is late. You would ask yourself about the meaning for you, and you would think positively. You would think, 'Great, I have another 10 minutes to answer my e-mails, and afterward I can really focus on the evening with my friend.' You need to shift from the victim to become an author."

Then John is silent. And I have too much to think about to speak.

We spend the whole day on the water, just sailing, enjoying nature. After a while, he speaks again, but only about mundane things. Then he lapses into a long silence again. It explains why he and my dad are friends. I have a lot to think about—capturing the hearts and minds of people—and how I can become an "author" and think positively more often.

CPO Best Practices

- To achieve a transformation, you need to win people's hearts and minds—then the rest will follow.

- Do not overly focus on meetings, schedules, and plans; people matter.

- Feel and act as the author of your life—not as the victim of situations and other people.

Chapter 14:
Too Simplistic

Heading back to Fort Wayne, I reflect on my weekend with John. I'm not sure that was the best way to spend my time. Enduring my parents' friends in their ridiculous Hawaiian shirts—in the fall at that—had tested my patience, especially in my current frame of mind. I still feel guilty about complaining to my parents as if I were a seventh grader. On top of that, Dad basically trapped me into hanging out with John. I really had wanted to talk to Dad. I know John's an old family friend, but it's not really his business.

Breakfast was nice, and hanging out on the boat was great—the weather was stupendous. But I'm not sure that John really knows what he's talking about. On the boat, his talk about the difference between playing the victim and being the master sounded plausible and reassuring. But now, sitting in my car driving back to reality, the effect is fading quickly. What difference does it make how I feel about being disrespected by Rick Fiore?

John's stories about Nueva Andalucía were great, but I don't see the connection to my own life. I'm just trying to get by at Heartland, not stage a revolution. And now I'm feeling guilty about leaving Heidi and the kids for the weekend.

As I stop at the oasis to fill up, I can't resist checking my iPhone. It's early Sunday evening, so I don't think that there will be a lot in my inbox. I'm surprised to see a message from John:

Thomas, it was good having you on the boat this morning. Hope you found our conversation useful. I know you are struggling with managing your emotions. It was hard for me 40 years ago when they taught me how in the service. And it has been hard on all the new recruits I pass it on to. What I can tell you, though, is that it works. To make it easier for you, you might want to answer the following questions for yourself:

1. *Why are you doing what you are doing, and what motivates you to be part of your current organization?*

2. *What do you expect from the people around you?*

3. *What are you willing to give to make the people around you successful?*

In my life, I've had my share of failures and disappointments. Every time I felt at the end of my rope, answering these questions helped me.

Best,
JMG

I am staring at my iPhone in disbelief. I spent the whole weekend getting some irrelevant questions from John? I'll have to tell Heidi about how I wasted the entire weekend. She won't be too happy. And tomorrow I'll face my team. The past 36 hours have been a complete joke.

I finally arrive home, and the kids are in their pajamas already playing on the living room floor. "Hi there, ready to go to bed already?"

"No Daddy, we've been playing here all day." I hear Heidi coming in the room and can't help but snap at her.

"Why didn't they get out all day? We have a big yard for Christ's sake!" Heidi glares at me for an eternity before motioning me to come into the den.

After closing the door she hisses: "How dare you, Thomas Sutter. You drag us to this godforsaken place, you are practically invisible the entire week, and then you spend the weekend in Chicago doing whatever you do there without even calling and the first thing you do when you come home is criticize me? Do you even care about what happens here? David has a cold and you know what happens when he coughs too much. He threw up in his bed at three in the morning. I spent an hour cleaning him up and the bed in the middle of the night. Then he came to sleep in our bed and threw up again. Not just in our bed but also in my hair. On top of that, I have an important meeting tomorrow that I need to prepare for. You're not the only one with a career, if you remember. So before I say anything in front of the children I might regret later on, why don't you get out of my face."

I don't know what to say, so I retreat to my study—cursing myself for being so rude and insensitive with Heidi. And yet I can't find the right words to apologize, it's never been easy with Heidi. Her strong will takes time to cool down. Maybe this could've been avoided if I hadn't fallen into the victim trap John was talking about!

Monday arrives, and the weather is awful—matching my mood. Heidi barely responds to my "good morning," and it takes all the resolve I have to drive to the office. Walking in, I feel like people are whispering about me. I try to ignore these thoughts as I head to my first meeting.

In the meeting I have trouble focusing. I'm thinking about too many other things: my fight with Heidi, Rick Fiore, last Friday's humiliation, and John's advice. If how I react internally to what happens really depends on my interpretation of the situation, how would that work? Yesterday, I was assuming that Heidi was giving the kids slack, while in reality she spent much of the day cleaning up David's mess. And today I feel even more miserable because people are whispering with each other. If I was in a better mood, would I have noticed that? As I start making a mental list of recent situations, I start to realize I could've had a completely different interpretation.

"Thomas, do you agree?" Gary Parker insists in a somewhat impatient tone. I manage to stutter something that sounds like "Sure go ahead," and suddenly I'm too hot. I'm a bit ashamed by my lack of focus at the meeting. Usually I have no problem paying attention, I even pride myself on my concentration. But it's been off since I got to Heartland. To avoid further humiliation, I attempt to put my worries and confusion aside and go through the usual series of back-to-back meetings reasonably okay. One resolution I make early on in the day though is to give serious thought to John's recommendations this evening. It won't hurt to try to answer those questions.

At four, I receive a text message from Heidi. "Will work late. Pls pick up the kids at 5:30. We need milk and bread and something for dinner. Luv Heidi." I look at the screen for a moment. The last part of the message is slightly encouraging—maybe Heidi has forgiven me, but it's hard to tell with her. Since Heidi started working, picking up the kids has become a challenge, even though they stay for the after-school program. This culture is so different from Dusseldorf. The expectation at her law firm here is to stay until eight at least a few nights a week and, if something is cooking, until midnight. This is daunting for Heidi. At least I have had a little more flexibility so far, but I will have to start going overseas soon. We really need a reliable babysitter. Maybe this is something I can do now to please Heidi.

I Google "Babysitters + Fort Wayne" and stumble over articles talking about a "trusted babysitter who had bludgeoned a 9-year-old Indiana girl to death with a brick and then dismembered her with a hacksaw." I lean back in my chair and attempt to remember how we found Ekaterina in the first place. I think she had been recommended by the neighbors. This will have to wait; I can't choose something so important in between meetings.

Picking up the kids is always nice. They come dashing out of school, their backpacks bouncing up and down. On the way home we stop at one of the huge grocery stores. Shopping here in the United States is so much nicer than in Germany. The stores are bigger, there are lots more varieties of products, the staff is friendlier and helpful, and they are open more often. Back in Dusseldorf everything is firmly closed on Sunday, but not so here.

We arrive home and I begin to prepare dinner.

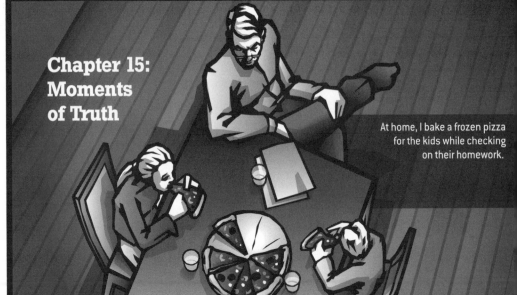

Chapter 15: Moments of Truth

At home, I bake a frozen pizza for the kids while checking on their homework.

Taking the kids to bed takes a bit longer than planned.

With the kids slumbering in their beds, I finally take time to look at John's questions once again.

I put the kids into the bathtub and apply the shampoo. While using the shampoo we make funny hairdos, which gets us all laughing.

I confirm that it was naïve to think these questions could change the world. I pour myself another glass of scotch and listen to the music.

At home, I bake a frozen pizza for the kids while checking on their homework. I don't make anything for myself. I've put on some weight, and the most effective way to lose it is to skip dinner. So I pour myself a Diet Coke and sit with the kids, watching them enjoy their pizza, and ask about their days. From time to time I force my mind back to listen to Johanna's and David's stories instead of drifting off to some of the many unsolved issues at Heartland. Putting the kids to bed takes longer than planned because apparently some kids at school have had lice, so we use a special shampoo as a precautionary measure. While using the shampoo we make funny hairdos, which gets us all laughing.

With the kids slumbering in their beds, I finally take time to look at John's questions once again to see if I have a different reaction:

1. *Why are you doing what you are doing, and what motivates you to be part of your current organization?*

2. *What do you expect from the people around you?*

3. *What are you willing to give to make the people around you successful?*

I put some jazz on the stereo, pick up a yellow notepad, and pour myself a glass of scotch. I write down my answer to the first question: "I am doing this for my family—for my kids in particular—to offer them a great and exciting life." That's obvious.

Reaching the second question, I write, "I want my team to contribute their creativity and ideas to meet to clearly exceed the savings target for the benefit of Heartland Consolidated Industries." And number three reads, "I am always going to go the extra mile for my team, working long hours, and dedicating weekend time to our joint mission."

After writing this down I am confirmed that it was naïve to think these questions could change the world. I pour myself another glass of scotch and listen to the music. My eyes wander over my notes again, getting stuck on my first answer: "… for my kids in particular—to offer them a great and exciting life." Suddenly I see myself at the dinner table earlier this evening, thinking about my earlier meetings while Johanna and David, full of excitement, were trying to share their adventures of the day with me. Then I see David fighting his cough over the weekend, throwing up more than once and Heidi cleaning up one mess after the other. I choke. As my mind goes further back in time, I see myself as a little boy with Mom and Dad at the table, eating, talking, joking…. Suddenly, I realized what actually mattered to me growing up—being with my parents, spending time with them, being loved and acknowledged by them. It didn't matter where we were. I stare at my answers and rip up the piece of paper so I can write down the true answers, and not the politically correct ones. This is a little intimidating, more than the twenty-minute exercise I thought I was getting into. I force myself to continue and write:

- I am here for the prestige of being the CPO of a multibillion-dollar company and striving to leave a legacy in turning Heartland's procurement upside down for the better.

- I expect my team to understand, accept, and appreciate modern practices in procurement, and to work harder to implement them.

- I am contributing the best of my expertise from the automotive world, which is at least a decade ahead of where Heartland is today.

I stare at my answers in front of me. Heidi sacrificed her advancing career in Germany, Johanna and David left their friends, all so I could follow my ambitions and gain prestige to impress people I don't even know. I can't decide if I am more embarrassed or shocked. I guess both. You never want to admit that you are as shallow and self-serving as the next guy. And everything else that should matter to me—global teams at work, success stories all over the place, and an active social life—I already had at Autowerke.

I rip these pieces up into even smaller pieces, creating a small mound in my trash can. I am beginning to understand how hard John's task actually is, and how these three questions are multidimensional. I am not going to give up though. I want to find out what I really need out of these questions. For Heidi and the kids too. Anyway, Heartland offered opportunities. Great ones, without any doubt! Now the pieces need to be put together—the things that really matter and the unique perspectives of Heartland.

After some painful moments of truth, I answer John's questions one last time, giving the *right* answers. And if they aren't true of my past, I will make them true of my future. Grabbing my MacBook, I open Word and start working. Taking easily over an hour, I finally produce something that satisfies me. As the clock rings in the new day, I review my answers one more time:

- I am with Heartland for a number of reasons. The first one is very mundane: I work here because I want to provide for my family. By providing, I mean offering opportunities to the kids. I want to give them the best education possible and show them the world. I want to do this through joint experiences, building strong family ties.

- The second reason for working at Heartland is making a difference. I have just read Steve Jobs's biography. He wanted to make a dent in the universe. Well, I am no Steve Jobs, but I really want my presence felt.

- The third reason is closely connected to the second. I like recognition. Being praised is something that really energizes me. My parents and especially my father knew how to get the best out of me by praising my achievements. At Autowerke, I got my fair share of praise consistently throughout my career there. I want to achieve the same at Heartland.

- The fourth reason is a tough one to write down. I truly like to be part of a committed team. I have always been a team player. In school, I was on several sports teams. At Autowerke, I first was part of a great team and afterward was allowed to build one. I believe that I like most of the people I have met at Heartland at a personal level. It just is so hard to generate some form of spirit here.

- Still, I feel motivated to work for Heartland—very motivated. Heartland is one of the world's greatest brand names. In fact, I grew up with Heartland products my parents bought at the Air Force base. Therefore, working for Heartland fills me with pride. Also, Heartland really has neglected its procurement function. I am convinced that I can have a really significant impact on helping Heartland to overcome the challenges it is currently facing.

- This brings me to the people around me. I expect them to

  - Be dedicated to their job.

  - Be loyal to Heartland.

  - Be open-minded.

  - Be willing to give their best.

  - Be honest and reliable.

- I am willing to make the people around me successful. In the past, I have always been able to strike a good balance between team success and personal success. At Heartland, I am willing to go one step beyond that. I am actually ready to let the team shine without standing in the limelight.

Looking at my answers, I think the third—that I like recognition—might need some more consideration. That one probably was one of the keys to success at Heartland. If I can really make the people in my group shine, this will make a huge difference. Before switching the MacBook off, I shoot a short thank you to John:

John:

Thank you for the time you spent yesterday and for your advice. It was very timely. I have observed myself twice in the victim cycle, once at home and once at work. Had I been able to manage my reaction by giving things a different interpretation—and thus being an "author," as you put it—I could've avoided a bad fight with my wife and provided for a happier and more effective day at work. I'll try to do better tomorrow. Also, I have worked on the questions you sent. Answering them has shown me one potential way to turn things around at Heartland. I suppose the answers are more for myself, but I've attached them anyway should you be interested.

Best,
Thomas

In the meantime, Heidi has come back home and sank into the sofa. I can tell by her silence that she isn't in the mood for talking. She surprises me by asking with a tired, but relaxed and somewhat joyful voice, "How was your day, Honey? Are the kids all right? We had a crazy day in the office—our case seemed to collapse, but then we crafted a different strategy and made it! The boss is happy, even called me in for a personal appraisal. How about a glass of wine before going to sleep?"

I relax. "Glad to hear you had a good day, my love. Heartland was business as usual. Regarding the kids, well … we have a pest alert. Otherwise everything is fine."

Heidi looks alarmed.

"Ha ha, no worries—the school found lice on one or two of the other kids. We have taken preventive measures. Everything's under control. And yes, a glass of wine would be great." While I open the wine, I look at Heidi, hesitate, but then ask, "How do you like Fort Wayne? I mean, I think you are doing a tremendous job, working long hours at the firm, on top of taking care of our new home, the kids. What drives you in doing all this for us? I mean, are you OK?"

"Maybe it's because I love you, sweet Tom Sutter? And because I know that you will not be happy with anything less than being the president of the United States or, if that is not possible, at least the president of Heartland….?"

"Um, well, thank you. But I'm serious. I mean, is there anything I can do to support you more?"

"Look, Thomas, I think Heartland is a big opportunity that you had to take. Had you not done it, you would have regretted it for the rest of your life, and we would have suffered with you. Actually, it *is* a great opportunity for *all* of us—particularly for the kids. They will be completely bilingual, and they will grow up in different cultures to become open-minded, great persons. This is more than worth the effort. For Johanna and David I want the best at any price."

"So do I," I say, this time convinced of my words. I sit down and rethink my whole exercise of the evening, looking over to see that Heidi has fallen asleep on the sofa. For a moment, I ponder carrying Heidi to bed as I used to. She usually would wake up and we would've taken advantage of the situation. But we aren't twenty-five anymore, and the kids are light sleepers, especially when they're sick. So instead I cover Heidi with a blanket, give her a kiss and sit there, wine in hand, watching her sleep. Yes I really love Heidi—and am so grateful for her support, and this moment of truth.

| CPO Best Practices |

- Be clear on your personal motivations:

  - Why are you doing what you are doing, and what motivates you to be part of your current organization?

  - What do you expect from the people around you?

  - What are you willing to give to make the people around you successful?

Chapter 16:
The Agenda

I don't get a lot of sleep.

Breaking my habit, I wake at 5:12 full of energy—and after many weeks of turbulence, finally with a plan.

And running is a great way to think it through before putting it into action.

I run for an hour and return home for a shower. I walk into the kitchen and turn on the coffee machine.

Coffee in hand, I walk over to my home office, switch on my computer, and start typing.

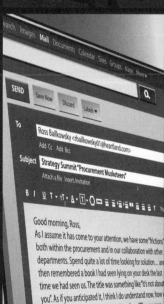

search Images **Mail** Documents Calendar Sites Groups Maps More▾

SEND   Save Now   Discard   Labels ▾

To   Ross Ballkowsky <rballkowsky01@heartland.com>
Add Cc   Add Bcc

Subject   Strategy Summit "Procurement Musketeers"
Attach a file Insert: Invitation

B I U ▾ T ▾ T ▾ A ▾ T ▾ ◯ ▾ ☰ ☰ ☰ ☰ ☰ ☰ ☰ ☰

Good morning, Ross,

As I assume it has come to your attention, we have some "frictions" both within the procurement and in our collaboration with other departments. Spend quite a lot of time looking for solution… and then remembered a book I had seen lying on your desk the last time we had seen us. The title was something like "it's not about you". As if you anticipated it, I think I do understand now, how we can make this change happen: Switching from "Thomas says…" "We believe…" where "we" is everyone in procurement, prod... R&D, Marketing, etc.

In the attached strategy paper I have sketched a detailed pl... 3-day Strategy Summit under the (working) title "Procurem Musketeers – All for One, One for All".

Here a brief summary:

Audience: All Procurement Staff from Fort Wayne, heads procurement from all major countries, Rick from produc... small team he chooses), Hernando Guardavilla from R&...

Tom W. Cane from Sales (+ team), Scarlet Ajtak from M...

I grab a tray, loading it with coffee, cereal, milk, and muffins, and walk upstairs to surprise Heidi with breakfast in bed.

I don't get a lot of sleep. Breaking my habit, I wake at 5:12 full of energy—
and after many weeks of turbulence, finally with a plan. It's still dark outside,
the sun doesn't rise until 7:30 or so, but I sneak out from the covers, pulling
on my gym shorts and sneakers. I creak the door open, carefully trying not to
wake Heidi.

And it's very cool—just above freezing. Soon I will teach the kids the
difference between 16°C and 61°F. I smile and start running. Sucking in the
cold, fresh air into my lungs feels good; my heartbeat echoes into my eardrums,
lifting my spirits. As I turn at the corner, my thoughts turn to putting my plan
in action: (1) Create a case for change, (2) Mobilize the stakeholders, (3) Train
the people, (4) Keep up momentum by recognizing and celebrating successes,
and (5) Become a true leader of this transformation through example.

I run for an hour, returning home for a quick shower. I walk into the
kitchen and turn on the coffee machine. Heidi and I fought about the ridiculous
prices for the coffee capsules, the procurement man in me twitching in
frustration. Even this can't spoil my good mood.

Coffee in hand, I walk over to my home office and switch on my computer.

06:48
From: Thomas Sutter
          <tsutter01@heartlandconsolidated.com>
To: Ross Bailkowsky
          <rbailkowsky01@heartlandconsolidated.com>
Subject: Strategy Summit "Procurement Musketeers"
Attachments: 120212_Strategy-Summit_v0.1 (concept).pptx

Good morning Ross,

I assume it has come to your attention that we have had some
"friction" within procurement and in our collaboration with
other departments. I have spent a lot of time looking for a
solution … and then I remembered a book I saw on your desk
the last time we had a meeting. The title was something like
It's Not About You. As if you anticipated it, I think I
understand now how we can make this change happen:
Switching from "Thomas says …" to "We believe …" where
"we" is everyone in procurement, production, R&D,
marketing, etc.

In the attached strategy PowerPoint, I have sketched a
detailed plan for a 3-day Strategy Summit under the
(working) title "Procurement Musketeers—All for One, One
for All."

Here is a brief summary:

Audience: All Procurement Staff from Fort Wayne, heads of local procurement from all major countries, Rick from production (plus a small team he chooses), Hernando Guardavilla from R&D (+ team), Tom W. Cane from Sales (+ team), Scarlet Ajtak from Marketing (+ team), Hugo Sebastian (IT)
Location: off premises
Date: in 2–3 weeks
Duration: 3 days
Agenda (preliminary):

Day	Time	Topic	Comment
I	8–9am	Working Breakfast	So most urgent daily business can get covered and we have increased chance of everyone actually being there by at the latest 9
	9–10am	Introduction (Ross/Thomas)	Would be great if you can come and share your thoughts and expectations of what procurement at Heartland should look like in one year, two years, five years
	10am–12pm	Team Building	Not easy in October/November but I remembered an activity we had in my earlier firm and found a provider offering this in Fort Wayne: **Cardboard Boat Building**
	12–1pm	Lunch	
	1–3pm	"Where is the Pain"	Everyone putting all cards on the table: what are the issues and challenges we are facing?
	3–6pm	Joint Vision	Vision & Mission Statement

Day	Time	Topic	Comment
2	8–9am	Working Breakfast	
	9–12pm	Workshop Carousel	Multiple break-out groups; everyone joins 4 of the 7 topics: Strategic Procurement Direct Materials Indirect Materials CAPEX Operational Procurement Materials Services Collaboration Procurement IT
	12–1pm	Lunch	
	1–5pm	Workshop Carousel (continued)	
3	8–9am	Working Breakfast	
	9–12pm	Presentation of Team Results	Would be great if you can join
	12–1pm	Lunch	
	1–2pm	Nomination of "Change Governors"	
	2–3pm	Wrap-Up	Would be great if you can provide a closing statement, kicking off the actual change and becoming reality

Hope this will find your support,

Thomas

Thomas Sutter
Chief Procurement Officer
Heartland Consolidated Industries, Inc.

I press the send button and hear that the kids are awake. I grab a tray, loading it with coffee, cereal, milk, and muffins, and walk upstairs to surprise Heidi with breakfast in bed.

CPO Best Practices

- Five steps are crucial to make a transformation happen:

  - Create a case for change

  - Mobilize the stakeholders

  - Train the people

  - Keep up momentum by recognizing and celebrating successes

  - Become a true leader through example

- Connecting people and building the team in procurement and across functions right at the beginning is a "must do" investment.

Chapter 17:
Go for Gold Is Born

The Europeans were generally receptive and curious. This is the first time they've seen initiative out of Fort Wayne. I really had a great time in Milan.

The Milan team was unlike the others he had seen anywhere else at Heartland so far. It started with the team leader there, an energetic lady named Laura Braida.

Besides the good results in Europe, my confidence is returning on a more solid foundation.

I'm sure Ross will give his full support, but I still have a lot prepared for my pitch.

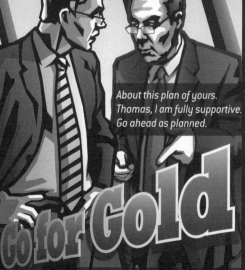

About this plan of yours. Thomas, I am fully supportive. Go ahead as planned.

Go for Gold

Following John's advice has done interesting things to my attitude.

By the way, Thomas, we need a name for this initiative. What about "Go for Gold"? Seems to sum things up pretty well don't you think?

These past two weeks have been interesting. On the surface, things around the office haven't changed much. I'm not part of the family yet and procurement people are still awkward around me, at least here in Fort Wayne. It was a different story in other locations—particularly European sites. I've just returned from the main non-German sites, all very far away from the politics in Fort Wayne.

The Europeans were generally receptive and curious. This is the first time they've seen initiative out of Fort Wayne. I really had a great time in Milan. Italy was always on my list at Autowerke. And the team there was quite a surprise. The team leader, an energetic lady named Laura Braida, in her early thirties, has a PhD in mathematics. Quite unusual for procurement.

We hit it off immediately. At lunch I entertained them with Autowerke war stories, such as our misunderstandings between the Essen headquarters and our Torino plants. Being a mathematician, Laura showed great interest in the cost regression analysis tool that Autowerke has in place. I told her I would send her the details on it.

Laura isn't the only great part of Milan. Her team members were a different breed than Fort Wayne. They seemed to be more open-minded and also have a better understanding of integrating manufacturing and engineering. Later I learned that our Milan division hired a lot of local talent from carmakers back in 2008. Maybe it's just me smelling the gasoline on them!

Besides the good results in Europe, my confidence is returning on a more solid foundation. Following John's advice has done interesting things to my attitude. I've stopped looking for praise and rewards and instead have my eyes focused on a long-term perspective. I also know where I want to take procurement, and how to get my people there. I don't quite get how exactly John affected me, and how three questions altered my focus so much. I have immense gratitude for him.

Due to flight delays out of Milan, I missed my connection from Chicago to Fort Wayne. I shower at O'Hare while waiting for the next flight, because now I have to go straight to the office for my meeting with Ross. I'm confident Ross will give his full support, but I still have a lot prepared for my pitch.

I arrive and sit outside Ross's office for long enough that Helen refills my coffee.

"Sorry to keep you waiting," she says. Ross should be available for you any minute now."

It turns into another twenty minutes before a group of people in expensive suits walk out of his office. Ross pats some backs in his jovial way, and then turns to me. "Thomas, come in, come in. I am terribly sorry for keeping you waiting for so long! The people you have just seen are investment bankers. We are discussing a—uh, confidential—acquisition that would strengthen our foothold in vitamins, supplements, and minerals. You know, sports nutrition and the like."

I think about my own approach to sports nutrition—freshly squeezed orange juice every morning and lots of pasta. I keep this thought to myself. Ross quizzes me about the trip to Europe and our procurement people over there. Ross is pleased with my report, so he turns to my proposal for the strategy summit.

"About this plan of yours. Thomas, I am fully supportive. Go ahead as planned and I will be there to address all the participants of this strategy summit. I like the term, by the way. We have not seen much strategy in procurement in the past. Do it somewhere special, too—maybe Mallorca would work. Would be an easy location for the Europeans as well, and also help everyone realize we are a global business. One thing though, you don't need to spend your late nights developing slides and proposals for me. I like to keep things informal at the leadership level. Next time you want to pitch something to me, just pop your head in and lay it out to me. Also, if you come by my office and the door is open, come in and have a coffee. It is always good to chat and exchange some ideas."

I make to leave, but Ross stops me. "By the way, Thomas, we need a name for this initiative. What about "Go for Gold"? Seems to sum things up pretty well, don't you think? Better than all these contrived initiative acronyms or basing the name on a university or famous person?"

"Makes sense, Ross."

As I leave Ross's office, I'm smiling. There are many cultural differences between Autowerke and Heartland—pitching to the CEO at Autowerke always required thorough preparation that had to be prevalidated ahead of time. Somehow, in this similarly large corporation, Ross has managed to be far more accessible and work without a large staff. His only staff is Helen, his assistant. He is clearly backing the initiative. Thinking all this over, my respect for Ross grows.

Chapter 18:
The Fight

The jet lag begins to hit me, so I call it a day and head home. I don't get a response from Heidi about picking up the kids, so I drive to the school. I see Heidi pulling out of the parking lot when I get there. I call her. "Hi honey, I'm right behind you. Didn't you get my message that I could pick up the kids? You could have stayed longer at the office for this case of yours."

"That's not necessary anymore," Heidi says in a flat voice.

"Why, what happened?"

"Tell you later," Heidi says and hangs up.

When I get home, the kids jump out and hug me. Heidi doesn't get out of the car. I usher the kids inside and then slide into the passenger seat of Heidi's car. "What is it, honey?"

"They have taken the case away from me and put Mark Sinclair in charge of it. Mark is barely out of law school and they've got me reporting to him."

"Why?"

"Well, you've been travelling all week and it was up to me to pick the kids up from school. Ralph, our boss, has the habit of arranging important milestone meetings at eight in the evening. I wasn't there twice in a row and he decided that I was not up to it."

"But why haven't you interviewed the babysitters I had contacted?" The moment these words leave my mouth, I know that it was a terrible mistake. I also recall that I contemplated calling my mother to see if she could spend the week in Fort Wayne while I was away, but I never followed up on the idea.

"Why? You have the nerve to ask me why? You're travelling around the world in one of these self-promotion tours of yours, leaving the kids and me alone in a place where a babysitter has just butchered a nine-year-old? How am I supposed to select the right candidate? I don't know anyone here. Ekaterina came to us on recommendation. I am not going to shop for someone who will be in charge of my children on the Internet."

"But the way things are will harm your career!"

"Looks like I don't have much of a career left anyway. I'm now reporting to a guy ten years my junior on a tiny case. And don't you pretend to be interested in my career. You're totally self-obsessed. At the slightest obstacle, you run whining back to your father as you've always done. At the same time, you trample over everything that is important to me. You have destroyed my career, my home in Dusseldorf, everything. What am I doing here? Tell me, why did you drag me out here?"

"But I want to be with you and the kids...."

"Oh really, when is the next long-haul trip on your agenda, tell me now!"

"It is ten days from now, and it will include the weekend."

"And to what terrible place will you have to go?"

I pause and stare out the window. "We will be going to Mallorca, staying in a beach resort, and sailing over the weekend for team building. Does this confirm your verdict that I am useless? I can see if my mother—"

"Thomas Sutter, this is not a game we are playing. You've let me down big time and you let the kids down. I am confused and need time to think. What I do know is that I want my life back, and I don't know what role you are supposed to play in it."

For the rest of the evening we avoid each other, even though I'm going away for the weekend. I have trouble falling asleep, but eventually jet lag wins.

Chapter 19:
Planning the
Strategy Summit

I'm driving out to the harbor to see John. I get up early to avoid any bad feelings.

I hop on the boat, store my luggage, and we push off.

During the cruise, I tell John about the plans I have in mind.

Time is moving quickly. After working really hard the past couple days, it's awesome to be on John's boat surrounded by such relaxing views.

• What is the personality of the interviewee?

• What really affects her/him (childhood, family, children, career, hobbies, etc.)?

• What are his dreams and ambitions?

• What prevents her/him from realizing or achieving them?

• Try to really understand the human being in front of...

● Why am I at this company? What motivates to be part of this organization?

● What do I expect from my colleagues within procurement/in different countries/in other functions?

● How do I contribute to this? What am I willing to give?

● This you would have never expect from me ...

I grab my new sailing bag from the trunk and a bag with food and beverages. John had suggested spending 2 to 3 days together to prepare the workshop.

I'm not keen on getting up this Saturday morning after my fight with Heidi. I'm driving out to the Chicago harbor to see John McGrath, a trip I had planned earlier in the week. I get up early to avoid any bad feelings. I'm wondering whether it would be wiser to stay home today, but I can feel that the atmosphere is still toxic. I conclude it's better to spend the day away.

It's strange, but I feel as if either my home life or professional life are in a good place, never both. It would be nice if I could be happy with both.

Ross's full support for my plan of conducting the strategy summit on a very nice island, including an expensive hotel with a great atmosphere is great—and it gives me confidence that Ross thinks I'm still the right guy for the job. He doesn't interfere, but rather wants to be kept informed. I park at the harbor, closing my door behind me ... and realize I left my keys in the car. Guess I was thinking too much about my agenda and plan for the summit. Luckily, the car wasn't locked yet, so I just take the keys out of the car.

Here's my plan so far: Ross is speaking first, laying out the overall plan of Heartland Consolidated Industries—strategy, importance of procurement, and goals for Heartland in the future. Then I will speak about our spend, the transparency we have, the lack of transparency in some of our Heartland countries in Europe, and about our achievements against maverick buying. Then I will present my plan for the future. To involve all the procurement staff from our countries, I will divide the group into 10 teams for workshops. Thanks to a number of phone calls with him recently, I've learned a lot from John about involving people, letting them make their presentations—bringing them to the front line. After three days, as an outcome of the meeting, I would like to have aligned sourcing teams and strategies.

I grab my new sailing bag from the trunk and a bag with food and beverages. John had suggested spending a couple days together to prepare the workshop. We will sail to a small, very quiet bay, where we don't have any cell phone coverage. John wants us to focus on what we are doing. He thinks the company's thoughts are in general too fragmented these days, and that nobody really focuses on things. I think about this a lot, for instance, when sitting in a phone conference already thinking about the next meeting or the supplier negotiation we have the next day; or when I was enjoying a wonderful meal, and not honoring the food but thinking about the next morning meeting. With a trip like this, John is helping me understand that I should enjoy life in the moment, not in the past and not in the future.

Furthermore, he's advised me to forget about my fear. Fear is only the imagination of something bad in the future. This prevents us from thinking about the current moment. I also brought a few bottles of red wine.

Arriving at the boat, John's already prepped everything to head out. I hop on, store my gear, and we push off.

"We're lucky we can go out this weekend," he says. "It's supposed to warm up nicely. Most of the other boats have been pulled from the water, but I'm always last out just so I can catch days like this."

I glance around and see that there are in fact very few boats in the water.

Cruising out of the marina, I describe my plans to John. But he just nods, in a "I understand your words" way, more than "I agree." A couple hours later we have reached our small bay—gorgeous, and no one's here. We set the anchor.

I think of Heidi, and how she would enjoy spending a weekend here.

John now has his iPad in front of him. "Thomas—this sounds ok to me. You do need to have some content for the meeting, but as it currently looks, it is very similar to what you have done previously, meaning it's all content, content, content. Instead, focus on the people. They are travelling to a nice and beautiful location. Most of them do not know each other, and you would like to change that. Try to make use of this and get their enthusiasm for the meeting to grow. For instance, use some place outside, a terrace or the beach of the hotel, and let them connect. Why should they sit in a basement without windows like in every other meeting you could do anywhere? Get their emotions going! So I would start with a meeting in the morning—and don't make it too early—where everybody can get to know each other. They should pair up in groups of two and interview each other. The questions should be very similar to what I sent to you when we met the first time. They should focus on the person, not on the work this person's doing. One question should be, why they are proud to be part of procurement? What they are passionate about in procurement?"

I ask John if he is serious. Does he really think people at Heartland are proud to be in procurement? I'm proud to be in procurement and to contribute to Heartland's financial results significantly, but I doubt that anybody else—except the Italians, my star group—are proud.

I say this very openly to John, who asks, "Thomas, how could you be successful with your people if they are not proud of what they are doing? Make them proud. Show them how important they are. These people are responsible for managing about 60% of the costs at Heartland. If they are successful, then Heartland is successful. If they fail, the company fails."

I think about my experience at Autowerke and compare it to Heartland. At Autowerke, people were really proud to be part of procurement. Procurement managers at Autowerke were self-confident because they knew that they had a major impact on the financial results of Autowerke. That gave them real power within the organization. The career path in procurement was very attractive there as well. The category directors at the headquarters were at the same salary levels as board members of one of Heartland's brands, with the same fringe benefits. My impression is Heartland has in recent years been offering procurement jobs to people who are too weak for marketing or not able to work in production any more. The contrast with Autowerke couldn't be bigger.

I explain this comparison to John, who just smiles and says that I got the point. "You should think about how to transform Heartland style into a style like Autowerke, without copying it. It is, after all, a completely different industry and culture."

The next day, John's up early and after a refreshing swim in the lake, we sit with a cup of coffee in the cockpit again. I tell John that I think the easiest thing would be for Dan Schaeffler to explain what the ingredients of Autowerke are that give procurement such a strong standing.

"That's a good idea Thomas—you should just do it. Invite him to the strategy summit. See if he'll give a speech about how Autowerke's procurement department managed to become so successful." I park this idea for now; I hadn't meant it seriously.

But he insists and continues. "Invite Dan, with his story on Autowerke, and try to get two to three other CPOs or CEOs as well to speak about their success in procurement. You can really learn from experiences of others, and having these people speak about their successes, but also about their obstacles they had to overcome, is quite a strong message."

I come back to the point: Which questions they should use for the "getting to know each other" interviews? John opens a file on his iPad and shows me the main objectives and questions to find out the answers:

- Your goal: To really understand the human being in front of you!

- What is the personality of the interviewee?

- What really affects him or her (childhood, family, children, career, hobbies, etc.)?

- What are his or her dreams and ambitions? What prevents this person from realizing or achieving them?

He explains that this is really getting to the human being and not just the job description. We discuss "being proud of procurement" again, and John swipes his iPad with more energy, coming to a headline: **Our Richness**.

"Thomas, in our society nobody dares to be proud anymore. Even the words proud and pride are considered by some people to mean arrogant, but they are not. If you are proud of something, it strengthens your personality and your passion. So we have to address their feelings of being proud with the questions. Ask them to reflect on the questions, to write the answers down for themselves, and then to exchange answers in pairs again, but mix up the pairs. Do not force them to say these answers in front of the group. If somebody wants to, fine, but do not force them."

Our Richness

- Why am I at this company? What motivates me to be part of this organization?

- What do I expect from my colleagues within procurement and/or in different countries and/or in other functions?

- How do I contribute to this? What am I willing to give?

- You would never have expected this about me: _____.

So we set the agenda for the first day of the meeting. This will be starting with Ross's speech and then will be focusing on team-building exercises, as well as addressing the questions we had just discussed. In the following hours we fix Day 2, the speeches that will be conducted by the three to four CPOs/CEOs and the same exercises as in Day 1, however, not only procurement but also the other functions. Day 3 will be the only content day in our strategy summit. We will discuss sourcing strategies and then kick off the category teams.

Time is moving quickly. After working really hard the past couple days, it's awesome to be on John's boat surrounded by such relaxing views. I am filled with energy. This is a new concept—to me and Heartland. It's a completely different style than what I've ever done in meetings and workshops before, and completely different from what I had in mind, but I feel very comfortable with the plan for the meeting. The only question is, will I be as compelling as John? He is able to cover the "people" parts very well and you really believe him. His charisma is fascinating. If I presented the same content without the "war" stories and the analogies, I would probably fail with this new concept and people would see me as "obscure Tom."

So I invite John to the summit; he's a bit reluctant at first because apparently he doesn't like speaking in front of so many people. It's interesting that John's one of the brightest guys I know and yet he is so shy.

CPO Best Practices

- Don't focus only on content—spend time to build the team.

- Think of the "team" expansively; it is wider than just procurement.

- Empower and challenge people to develop their own solutions to problems; don't just "dictate" the answer.

Let me share a secret with you. Why am I doing this? Because I trust you. And because I trust in you. Heartland has made mistakes. I have made mistakes.

I have a vision for Heartland. For our new Heartland. And you are a central part of it. Actually, I want to build this together with you.

We want to be open minded and learn from others – inside and outside the company.

I want you to be able to say that Heartland procurement is the best place you have ever worked.

Mallorca. An unusually mild and sunny Thursday morning for this time of year. The light breeze coming in from the sea is gently caressing the faces of Heartland's procurement staff whom I am watching. They are sitting—not all of them perfectly at ease—in the stylish meeting room of the modern 5-star hotel my assistant booked for the summit. The glass front of the room has been removed, virtually turning the conference area into part of the sea-facing terrace where groups of lounge furniture are scattered around here and there, accompanied by small tables offering a variety of seasonal fruit and local snacks. The podium is arranged where the glass doors had been before, inviting the audience to let their eyes wander from the speaker to the terrace, reflecting the golden morning light, to the breathtaking view of the deep blue sea, framed by a rocky, maquis-covered coast and decorated with a handful of white, slowly moving sails.

Ross Bailkowsky, wearing a blue polo shirt over white trousers, is casually standing in front of his people without projector, without microphone. I have introduced John to Ross, and we've briefed him on the intended outcome of the meeting. Once he starts to speak—slowly and with well-placed pauses—it's clear he understood our intent completely.

"Good morning—and a very warm welcome to all of you. To each *one* of you. I am very happy that you have all accepted the invitation to come to this, well, slightly remote place, and it fills me with pride to see what an impressive group has gathered here. Let me first ask you a question: Have you been swimming this morning? Who of you has already been out swimming?"

[Silence.]

"OK, who went for a little run along the coast and saw the amazing sunrise?"

[Some people clear their throats.]

"I see…. Did anyone take a walk down to the harbor to watch the fishermen come in with their catch of the day?"

[No response.]

Ross isn't the least bit flustered. "All right, come on. Show me your hands: Who has been doing any one of these things or has in any way taken advantage of this beautiful location for some kind of pleasant activity?"

[A few hesitant hands rise.]

"OK. Some of you went out and had some fun. Well done! This is one of the main reasons why we are here…."

[Whispering all around.]

"Many of you will certainly have asked yourselves, 'Why the hell have they pulled me out of—wherever—to get to this island somewhere in the Mediterranean Sea?' Well, the main reason for this is that we should have some fun. Actually, we should have more fun in *anything* that we are doing. Together as a team. And to give everybody a fair chance to start tomorrow with some pleasant activity, we will postpone the start of tomorrow's agenda by one hour. Use the time to go out, use it to enjoy! I'm not kidding!"

[People exchange incredulous glances.]

"And there is something else about this island. Officially, for *some* reason, some other place somewhere out there in the sea has earned the title of being the 'Heart of the Mediterranean.' I don't care. To me, the heart of the Mediterranean Sea is here. In *this* place. And for *many* reasons, it's also the heart of our company. Heartland's heart will be beating in this place exactly for the next three days. Joyfully. Strongly."

[Silence, absorbed by the distant sounds of the sea.]

Ross lowers his voice, "Let me share a secret with you. What I will now be saying, you will never hear from me anywhere else again after this meeting. Why am I doing this? Because I trust you. And because I trust *in* you. Heartland has made mistakes. I have made mistakes. Our results last year have disappointed the financial world, and some people out there even blame us for making people sick from unhealthy nutrition. This hurts me, and I know that it hurts you as well. Now, what have been the mistakes? Our mistakes as a company are that we have been focusing, for too long, too much, on ourselves. This caused us to miss important trends in the market, trends in a changing world around us.

"Heartland has become too reliant on its long heritage of products—old products that have been good and successful, for sure. But we have not taken the energy to explore other, new product segments like health food, which is now a strongly growing market. Growing against the trend. And health food could help make a difference in the world for the better."

Ross pauses, then tells the group that Heartland, as an organization, has become too self-reliant, too content on doing things the good old way, the way it has always done things. He says the organization has missed new, better practices, which explains why, suddenly, its competitors have overtaken the company.

He tells the group that everyone, himself included, has become too self-satisfied with "ourselves and our little kingdoms," and that this has resulted in losing track of each other and the team's ability to hear new ideas.

"But that," he says emphatically, "is the past."

[Silence.]

Ross raises his voice. "I have a vision for Heartland. For our *new* Heartland. And you are a central part of it. Actually, I want to build it *together with you.* We will make a difference. We as a team will make a difference in our company, and Heartland as a company will make a difference in the world!"

I glance over at John, who returns a subtle nod. I smile.

Ross then tells the group about the company's new goal to market products that contribute to people's health and welfare, and about the company's new commitment to helping provide the underprivileged in the world with healthful food. He explains how the company will do business in these markets: by working with local firms and buying more of the host country's raw materials.

"So, do we not want to make money anymore? Of course we do! But we also want to make a difference and demonstrate social responsibility. If we do this well, we will even make money *out of* this—for the benefit of Heartland *and* for the welfare of the societies in the world.

"With regard to the way we do business, we want to be open-minded and learn from others—inside and outside the company. By not wasting our time, either by not progressing or by reinventing everything all over again, we will be so much more powerful in anything we do—if we are open to share, take, and build on what is already out there, focusing our efforts on the missing things. By the way, I personally have already learned a lot from this gentleman over there," points at me, "and I know that I will be learning even more from *you all* while building Heartland toward our new vision.

"With regard to the people ... to us ... I want us to become *one* team, in procurement and beyond. We will forge this group of great individuals," and here he gestures at the whole audience, "into one single, even greater team. A team that has the trust in each other to share, that has the confidence to praise each other, and that has the pride to celebrate the joint successes together. A team that will make a difference at Heartland—and in the world!"

Small drops appear on Ross's forehead, sparkling in the morning light. I glance around to see if people have the telltale smirk of the cynic on their faces. None do.

Ross says this vision of the future Heartland will never come true, however, without billions of productivity gains that he promised Wall Street, savings created by procurement, which will supply the funds to build its business around the new strategy.

He holds up one finger. "Innovation: The biggest pool of innovative ideas is not within our company—but the labs and engineering departments of our suppliers are an inexhaustible source of ideas, for new ingredients, for more attractive or functional packaging, for more efficient production equipment. Let's harness this innovation power to drive Heartland's success, to drive our success."

He holds up a second finger. "Passion: It would be a waste of your time, of your intellectual power, if we continued having you spend one month every year on the annual negotiations with your individual suppliers and then another eleven with administration and other operational work. You as a team are managing 60% of Heartland's cost base! You are the gatekeeper to Heartland's biggest innovation pool! Driving Heartland's value by managing this is the purpose of our new procurement. This is your purpose as a team. Such purpose drives passion, passion drives success ... and success drives fun. I want you to have fun. I want you to be able to say that Heartland procurement is the best place you have ever worked! And I want you to be able to say that you *cannot think* of any other better place to work. I want you to drive Heartland's success. I want you to be the heart of our company. I want you to be Heartland's heart that starts beating here on this beautiful island over the next three days before it will continue beating everywhere in our company."

I look over, and now John is sporting a big grin. I've never seen him do that. He sees me and gives me a thumbs up.

Ross takes a breath. "I want us to be successful as *one* team. I give you my commitment to bringing this vision into reality. I would like you to think of your commitment—as part of *one* team—over the next few days. And even if the only thing we take home from this summit is growing together as a team, knowing not only each other's' names and phone numbers, but also each other's faces and the people behind them, we will have accomplished more during three days than we have through anything else over the past three years.

"Now let me hand you over to Thomas, and—please—enjoy the beauty! Thank you."

There are moments of silence, everybody seems overwhelmed, and then resounding applause.

CPO Best Practices

- Demonstrating top management commitment is a crucial enabler for a transformation.

- Showing respect to the staff and making them feel it is one of the greatest motivators.

- Disclosing selected personal weaknesses and strengths builds trust.

Chapter 21:
Getting Into It

Now let me hand it over to Thomas.

Tom – it's all yours now.

Dear colleagues, after such a speech, it is difficult to find the right words. Let us in Procurement grow together as one team.
To guide us on this way, I have invited a John McGrath to facilitate this first day of our summit.

I suggest that we do not lose too many words and time about me. Because this summit is all about you as a team ...

After this emotional roller coaster ride for the audience, John points out that it is time to start getting into it and to get to know each other much better.

Heartland's procurement staff is totally absorbed by John's speech, and fascinated by his vigor and the precision of his messages.

At the end of the day, what was a group of people are on their way to becoming a team of partners, and the long networking dinner on the terrace is followed by an even longer evening at the bar.

Ross invites me to the podium with a handshake, patting me on the back: "Tom, it's all yours now." He walks to the back, taking a seat somewhere in the crowd. Now I'm alone in front of the group, unsure whether I'm overwhelmed or insecure. But the adrenaline rushing in my veins takes control, and I look over at John who is now sitting in the front and nodding. I look at the audience, take a deep breath, and start:

"Thank you, Ross. Dear colleagues, after such a speech, it is difficult to find the right words. I'm impressed. I am deeply impressed with two things: first, this amazing group of people. Thank you for coming to this place literally from all over the world. I know that many of you had to put down other priorities to make this happen. Again, thank you very much for this, and welcome! Second, I am impressed with Ross's great, great demonstration of commitment to us as a procurement team, and to our new role within Heartland. This is more than most procurement organizations out there in the world can ever dream. It's a huge responsibility, and it's a big opportunity for us at the same time. Seeing you all here together, I am sure we can do it."

I remind them that Ross mentioned three things that, going forward, Heartland needs to do better than in the past: managing product strategy, our way of working, teaming up more effectively. I tell them this means

(1) Fulfilling our new, big role with regard to cost reduction, innovation, and many other types of value contribution.

(2) Collaborating and learning from each other, and from others both inside and outside Heartland.

(3) Growing together as a team and building strong networks, again inside and outside Heartland.

"With this strategy summit," I say, "we want a great leap ahead on this agenda. So, what exactly is it that we plan to do here? Well, let me do this in reverse order." I then lay out the next three days, beginning by saying that the job of fulfilling our new role as procurement professionals within Heartland will start as soon as we get back from the summit. We will, however, take some time on Day 3 to develop the first cornerstones of our future category strategies.

I tell them that our new job of learning from others will happen on Day 3, with presentations by some of the most successful and respected CPOs in the world. These three heavyweights from very different industries will talk to the group about their challenges in transforming procurement in their companies and how they mastered them.

Then I tell them that laying the fundamentals for better collaboration with our internal customers will start tomorrow, Day 2, when some of the key stakeholders from other parts of the company will join the summit. This, I say, will be a great opportunity to get closer to them as a cross-functional team, and to create a better mutual understanding of joint needs, expectations, ambitions.

"But first, today actually, or more precisely, right now, let us start with the most important part: Let us in procurement grow together as one team. To guide us, I have invited John McGrath to facilitate this first day of our summit. John has worked for many, many years in key positions in public service and has experience in dealing with people, teams, and organizations. Please welcome John, who might also want to introduce himself a little more."

Courteous applause as John approaches the stage. Calmly, he focuses on the people in the audience one by one, picking them at random. Just by standing there in front of the crowd, John somehow manages to project an amazing charisma, which immediately gets everybody's attention. "Thank you for the warm welcome. I suggest that we do not waste too many words and time on me. Because this summit is all about you as a team...."

John delivers a wonderful speech about organizational transformation, particularly pointing out the emotional elements of it; talking about the importance of building personal relationships and the need to establish a collaboration culture that puts the team's success above individual aspirations, and about the concept of becoming the author of your life. Heartland's procurement staff is totally absorbed by John's speech, fascinated by his vigor, the precision of his messages, and the astonishing relevance of all his anecdotes.

After this emotional roller coaster ride for the audience, John points out that it is time to start getting into it and to get to know each other much better. For this exercise, John asks the crowd to break out in groups of ten (randomly picked beforehand) and form five pairs within each group. In pairs, people are asked to interview each other using the questions that John and I developed on our boat trip. The last question is particularly important, he says, asking everyone to share one little-known secret about themselves. John has found many times that offering a very personal, in some instances maybe even a little bit delicate fact or experience, often does an amazing job in breaking barriers and building bridges between people. After the interviews, everybody is asked to introduce their partner to the rest of the respective group and finally, each group will be, on a voluntary basis, invited to share the statements that mattered most to them with the group.

John tells the groups to go off and find a nice spot anywhere around the area. The time given for the exercise is much more than needed to complete the task. The idea is to make it as easy as possible to get people engaged in personal conversations beyond the given agenda. Having come to the summit with the expectation of getting forced into some small air-conditioned meeting rooms with artificial light to do number crunching work and dig into each other's sourcing practices, everybody is bluntly surprised with the agenda for the day. Some of Heartland's procurement staff enters the terrace with its lounge corners, some discover the deck chairs in the pool area, and some even conquer the small beach belonging to the hotel, sitting in the sand.

Everywhere, people are introducing themselves, discussing the questions, or just chatting business and life in general over a cup of coffee and some snacks.

When everybody gathers again, the group is not the same compared to the one in the morning. All the uneasiness is gone; everybody looks upbeat and energized. Small groups, many of them with people from different sites and geographies walk in, chitchatting, joking, being themselves. This time, John has a hard time making himself heard, and when he asks for the most relevant statements, dozens of arms go up immediately to share. John captures some by writing them on a flip chart.

In the afternoon, John has the group do a few training exercises. At the end of the day, what was just a group of people are now on their way to becoming a team of partners, and the long networking dinner on the terrace is followed by an even longer evening at the bar.

| CPO Best Practices |

- Sharing a vision that everyone can buy into is a critical transformation ingredient.

- Building the team is absolutely crucial.

- "Work" does not always need to feel or look like "work."

Chapter 22:
Building Bridges

Despite a short night, quite a few people follow Ross's advice to use the time before the meeting to do something nice.

Some groups are meeting for a run, others improvising a yoga session on the beach, and others just enjoying the sunrise during a little walk or over early morning tea sitting on a deck chair.

When their stakeholders, who had been invited to the summit from the second day on, arrive ...

... they find a relaxed crowd that seems to have known each other for a long time.

HEARTLAND INC.
FORT WAYNE, INDIANA, U.S.A.

Procurement Strategy Summit 2012

■ Why am I at this company? What motivates me to be part of this organization?

■ What do I expect from my colleagues in procurement/ in different countries/ in other functions?

■ How do I contribute to this? What am I willing to give?

■ This you would never expected from me ...

Rick finds the other blue tag with a circle, lets his eyes wander up—and looks into mine.

OK, come on — let's get it done.

Our forced interview turns into a completely personal conversation.

After dessert, I take a few minutes for myself and sit down.

At quarter past seven, the bus departs with everyone in a relaxed and upbeat mood. We finally descend on a small bay with a traditional fish restaurant at the bottom.

I'm very happy with the summit so far, but I can't help thinking of Heidi.

Despite a short night, quite a few people follow Ross's advice to use the time before the meeting (which has indeed been pushed ahead by one hour—Ross kept his word) to do something nice. Over the last round at the bar, many made plans for the next morning, which made it difficult to just sleep in again. I think team dynamics may be winning over individual laziness.

I ponder the participants as I fight putting on my running clothes. Some groups are meeting for a run, others improvising a yoga session on the beach, and others just enjoying the sunrise during a little walk or over early morning tea sitting on a deck chair.

Heartland Consolidated Industries
Procurement Strategy Summit
2012

Agenda, Day 2

- Opening and welcome of the extended team
  10:00–10:15
  Thomas Sutter

- Building Heartland's supply management network
  10:15–12:30
  John McGrath

  Lunch break   12:30–2:00

- Supply management ambitions and priorities
  2:00–5:45
  Gary Parker

- Wrap-up of the day
  5:45–6:00
  Thomas Sutter

  Departure to dinner location   7:30

Well before the start of the official agenda at 10:00, most of the procurement people are already busy talking on the terrace. When their stakeholders from production, R&D, IT, and the business functions, who've been invited to the summit from the second day on, arrive, they find a relaxed crowd that seems to have known each other for a long time. Surprised and feeling a little bit like the new joiners to the party, they keep themselves busy searching for a cup of coffee or a croissant while Ross and I do our best to shake hands and bring them up to speed. I can see John watching as I extend a very short welcome to Rick Fiore, avoiding direct eye contact, and then quickly rush to welcome Hugo Sebastian from IT with warmth. John gives Rick a blue nametag with a circle printed on the right side.

Once everybody has successfully been ushered to the conference area, I open the meeting with a special welcome to the new participants. I give what I feel is a warm speech, describing how, going forward, procurement is planning to collaborate in partnership with the other functions, and how we intend to become much more transparent about roles and responsibilities. Afterward, the same introduction procedure from yesterday starts, only now it includes people from non-procurement functions. This time, the group is split by category teams and mixed with their respective stakeholders. Today, the pairs are already predefined by the color and printed symbol on name tags to ensure maximum cross-functional interaction.

After some search, Rick finds the other blue tag with a circle, lets his eyes wander up—and looks into mine. After a moment of silence, it's Rick who says, "OK, come on—let's get this done." We find a calm spot away from the others and do our mutual interview professionally but halfheartedly, trying to keep things rather short. Here are Rick's answers:

Our Richness

- Why am I at this company? What motivates me to be part of this organization?

  - Great company with a great tradition

  - Responsibility for Heartland's core operations, which is the source of the company's productivity, income and profit, and which is ultimately the purpose of its existence

- What do I expect from my colleagues within procurement/in different countries/in other functions?

  - Provide service and support to Heartland's core operations to ensure smooth processes for minimization of downtimes and maximization of high-quality output

- • Prioritize Heartland's productivity over any other targets, as productivity drives the company's—and our—incomes

- • How do I contribute to this? What am I willing to give?
  - • I am dedicating all my passion and time to keep our production running
  - • I am accessible for my team whenever needed, 24/7

- • You would never have expected this about me:
  - • I have a procurement background, having headed our purchasing department in Italy 15 years back

At the end of mine, I mention neutrally that my family is still trying to get settled in Fort Wayne, and it's important for my kids to make friends and get integrated. Rick, who can't deny his Italian roots, asks out of genuine interest how they're doing, how they like the United States, etc. I mention some challenges at home, such as our difficult search in finding a babysitter due to the recent murder. Rick, who has two little twin girls of his own and understands my situation very well, offers their own babysitter, who they've been using for a long time. He also says that his family, especially his wife, who is originally from San Diego, has found it very hard to build up—and to like— their life in Fort Wayne, and they've had quite a few arguments over this. I bluntly look at Rick, stunned by his openness. In return, I talk about Heidi and her many frustrations, the fights we've been having, and more. Our forced interview turns into a completely personal conversation—discovering we even have a lot of similarities. We almost forget the time and have to be called twice to rejoin the team to do the introductions: I'm feeling much better now, and I think Rick is too.

In the afternoon, Gary Parker, who has developed tremendously during the past months, virtually becoming my right hand, facilitates the Black Hat/ White Hat exercise to develop a joint document with procurement's internal customers on the supply management ambitions, priorities, and needs at Heartland.

For this purpose, the group is split into the "White Hats" who have the task of coming up with ideas of what should be done, changed, and improved in terms of strategic direction; ways of working together in supply management for Heartland's benefit; and how to best comply with the responsibility that Ross has put on procurement's shoulders in his opening speech. The "Black Hats" have to play the devil's advocate in identifying all the effort required, the risks, and the worst-case scenarios. Afterward, the points from both groups are put on the table, discussed, and balanced. The final result is a joint, cross-functional document detailing commitments on priorities and actions. As part of this, R&D gives its commitment to dedicate resources to purchasing-related activities, which is a major breakthrough, given the previously strained relationship between the two departments.

At quarter past seven, the bus departs with everyone in a relaxed and upbeat mood. We drive for almost an hour on a winding road, following the rocky coast of the island, to finally descend on a small bay with a traditional fish restaurant. Tables have been arranged outside on the terrace, providing a beautiful view of the beach, framed by cliffs on both sides. The group is enjoying the mild evening, engaging in conversations that continue the whole evening, about activities of the day, the summit so far, business going forward, and life in general. The atmosphere is so informal that people even stand up between courses taking a few minutes for a talk standing on the terrace or on the beach.

After dessert, I take a few minutes for myself and sit down in one of the deck chairs on the beach. I listen to the small waves licking the sand, watch the moon and the twinkling stars over the beautiful bay, and I fill with melancholy. I'm very happy with the summit so far, but I can't help thinking of Heidi. She would've adored this place. However, our lives have changed. If she pictures me in this place, I will get the blame for going on vacations without her. I then bitterly remember that we have already passed even this stage, and at this point we are barely speaking. Is it possible to be successful in business and have a happy family life at the same time? Its pale light glittering on the water, the moon had built a silver bridge toward Thomas.

| CPO Best Practices |

- Making promises—and keeping them—builds credibility and trust.

- Ideas and opportunities as well as doubts and risks must be brought up and discussed openly to avoid hidden resentments spreading.

Chapter 23:
Route to Nirvana

I set the alarm for six in the morning on Day Three of the strategy summit. Judging by the informal feedback I've received and also by my own impressions, the first two days had been a success.

I have to leave this session in order to welcome our guests.

I hear something. It's the unmistakably rough sound of Autowerke's V10 engine powering the signature Italian super cars.

Three **V10s race up the** long driveway of the hotel at a reckless speed.

Dan sends a text massage to meet them in front of the hotel.

Despite two short nights in a row and my jet lag, I set the alarm for six in the morning on Day 3 of the strategy summit. I don't want to lose the routine of daily runs. Judging by the informal feedback I've received and also by my own impressions, the first two days had been a success. Ross Bailkowsky and John McGrath made Day 1 really special. I had expected Ross to be an excellent speaker and wasn't disappointed by his performance in front of the procurement team. He had elegantly woven the success of procurement into the overall story to transform Heartland. Had stock analysts been present during his speech, Heartland's share price would have taken a big leap.

The real surprise has been John, though. Asking for his help to prepare the strategy summit had been a no brainer, but asking him to facilitate large portions of the meeting was a little risky. After all, John is not a man of many words. On stage, John underwent some kind of metamorphosis. He appeared to glow from within. While John spoke, the room was absolutely silent, all eyes were fixed on him. He still spoke slowly, in short sentences, and his voice seemed to have gained some kind of hypnotic effect. With his introduction speech, John had almost single-handedly secured the success of the strategy summit. All the usual skepticism and cynicism that I learned to accept as an unwelcome reality at all meetings I had attended throughout my professional life had all but vanished.

Day 2 had been a personal victory for me. Finally mending fences with Rick Fiore meant a lot. I'm certain that Day 3 will be just as good as the preceding ones. Today will see the launch of global category teams. I hope this important milestone will leave a lasting memory for participants. I still remember John's words: "Don't waste the precious time you have with people who flew in from all over the world with standard presentations. All of that can be dealt with later via conference calls. Do something special, something that will truly inspire people. In your trade, who do you admire most?"

I have to admit it is Dan Schaeffler, the CPO of Autowerke. John insisted that I call Dan and invite him to give a speech at the strategy summit. Initially, I was very reluctant to do so. After all, I quit on Dan, and hadn't spoken to him since leaving Autowerke. All of this still seemed too fresh. "All the more a reason to call him," John said. "You cannot hide from your past, Thomas. It is important that you be totally at ease with yourself. Don't give yourself an excuse to let your mind wander back to the past and question the decisions you took then. These would be distractions. I need you to be able to focus on the present 100%."

I didn't have a way out. I chose the easy way and dropped Dan an e-mail. Five minutes later, my phone rang. Dan was just as warm as ever, and very eager to hear the latest. He also immediately agreed to speak at the strategy summit ("No problem, as long as you don't work for one of Autowerke's competitors") and even offered to take along two other CPO acquaintances of his.

I stop running to enjoy the start of the beautiful sunrise over the sea. This is actually my first trip to Mallorca. I believed Mallorca to be an overcrowded tourist spot, and am truly amazed at how beautiful it is off the beaten tracks. I do some yoga before walking back to the hotel.

The formation of the category teams proceeds nicely and as smoothly as expected. Gary Parker does a solid job facilitating that session. I think it's interesting how Gary has changed over the past couple months. He's turned from being extremely cold, bordering on hostile, to one of the people I rely on most.

I have to leave this session to welcome our guests. Dan offered to fly the other two associates down to Mallorca on his corporate jet ("After all, they are my suppliers").

Dan sends a text message to meet them in front of the hotel. Curious about what Dan is up to, I step out in the open into the warm Mediterranean sunshine. There are no cars in sight. On the verge of calling Dan to see what is going on, I hear something. It's the unmistakably rough sound of Autowerke's V10 engine powering the signature Italian super cars along the winding streets of Mallorca's countryside. Not one but two, no, three of them! The bellowing of the engines grows louder and louder, and I can see a long cloud of dust marking the road to the hotel. Finally I see the cars; three V10s race up the long driveway of the hotel at a reckless speed and come to a screeching halt right in front of me. The gull-wing doors open and Dan jumps out of the first car and shakes my hand with genuine delight. "Thomas my friend, here come the three musketeers at your rescue," Dan smirks. "Meet my friends Luis-Pierre Weinmann from Pan Euro Télécom and Mark Ellis from Am-Alu Forge in Pittsburgh."

"Welcome gentlemen, pleasure to meet you. Thank you so much for being here. Dan, what style to show up in!" By now, a small crowd has gathered to peer at the cars.

"Well, I thought I'd give the boys a treat. The V10s are here anyway for a promotion tour with the press. I just borrowed them from the marketing tour for today. And I tell you what, that car has been built for streets like these. Driving them on a German autobahn is a waste."

I take Dan, Luis-Pierre, and Mark up to a terrace overlooking the foothills of the Serra de Tramuntana mountains. We have olives, cheese, and local bread and later delicious pastries. I brief the three CPOs on the type of audience they will meet and on the general mood in the meeting. Dan is visibly looking forward to his speech. "Thomas, don't you worry about our speeches. I have known Luis-Pierre and Mark for many years now, and we have spoken together at conferences many times in the past. You and your people will find them interesting, since we took very different approaches to procurement and still delivered comparable results. Am I right here?" he asks, turning to Luis-Pierre and Mark. Both agree. I don't quite understand what it is with these different approaches, and I didn't know of the friendship among the three CPOs, but I make a mental note that going forward I also need to build a network with CPOs of other companies.

The three CPOs are a great success. They obviously have done this together before, and they tease each other in front of the audience. Everybody has a really good time. Only John is taking notes, frowning, and going back to his material. At the end of the session Dan, Luis-Pierre, and Mark receive a thundering round of applause. Bidding them goodbye, I say, "Guys, if you ever grow tired of procurement, you may want to consider an alternative career as stand-up comedians!"

The not-surprising unison response is, "We have thought about it many times!"

On my way back into the meeting, I'm intercepted by John: "So what did you think about the speeches?" he asks.

"Well, I believe these guys are just great. Consider that between the three of them they are responsible for a procurement spend north of $150 billion, yet they are funny, playful, and entertaining. To me, all three are role models. I aspire to be like one of them five years from now."

"Which one of them?"

"What do you mean? All three are really successful. But if I had to choose, I would like to be as successful as Dan Schaeffler."

"That's not what I meant. You did not really listen to what they said, did you? If you had listened, you would have heard three very different stories. Yes, all three of them have reached what Dan Schaeffler has called the Nirvana of procurement, but they got there on three very different routes, didn't they?"

I'm confused. I say, "Well, I remember Dan saying something about them having taken very different approaches. But all three of them went for savings and changed the organization ... they work in different industries—is this what you are talking about?"

John's look comes close to disgust. "Look, I am not a procurement expert, but I heard something that I consider very relevant for your immediate task. What I heard was that all three of them are breaking down procurement into two major directions. One is external effectiveness. This one encompasses everything you are doing to get more out of your suppliers. The other direction is internal effectiveness. This one is all about getting your act together within procurement but also about collaboration with other internal functions like engineering."

While talking, John draws a rectangle on his iPad. "See, the horizontal dimension stands for external effectiveness and the vertical dimension stands for internal effectiveness. When Dan, Louis-Pierre, and Mark started ten or fifteen years ago, they found their organizations down here at the lower left-hand side corner. That's exactly the position you and Heartland find yourselves in."

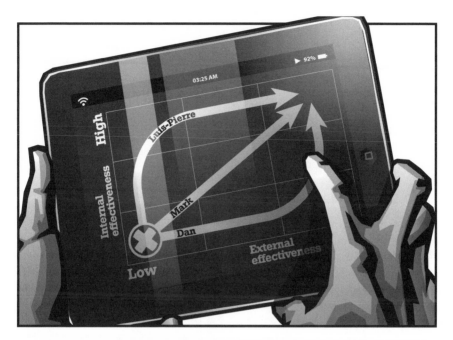

John draws a fat X in the lower left hand side corner of the rectangle.

"Now, Dan Schaeffler at Autowerke headed off straight to the right. He went for savings first. Remember, fifteen years ago, Autowerke was in a financially very difficult situation. So Dan did everything to drive down cost with suppliers. He was lucky in a way then because he could come up with lots of new tools like this cost regression thing that took suppliers by surprise. By driving down cost so rigorously, he gained the respect of his peers in the other functions. He then changed the way procurement operated at Autowerke, meaning he moved up on this chart."

He draws a curved arrow, starting off horizontally and then taking a sharp bend upwards. "Louis-Pierre Weinmann was in a very different situation at Pan Euro Télécom ten years ago. In the high growth years of the mobile phone business, the company was very profitable then. Being French, they were very good at doing strategies and forecasting market developments. So they understood earlier than everybody else that the party would not last forever. So he started working on the excellence of procurement. He diligently worked on processes, guidelines, and capabilities. So he started moving straight up. When profits at Pan Euro Télécom started to decline, Louis-Pierre's time had come. He had everything ready and took off on a flying start." John's finger draws another curved arrow, this time starting vertically and then bending right.

"Mark Ellis was facing the toughest challenge five years ago. Am-Alu Forge was in trouble, and he had to deliver right from start. So he had to fix the plane and fly it at the same time. What was good for him was to have the full-hearted support of the CEO. See, he took the direct route."

John draws a diagonal arrow from the lower left-hand side corner upward. He smiles proudly. "Makes sense?"

"Wow, John, I have to admit you play in a completely different league. How do you come up with these things? And yes, absolutely, this makes a lot of sense. This is what Dan had been hinting at. But obviously he wanted me to work it out myself. I am glad you were here to do it for me."

"You can do this yourself Thomas. You just need to be 100% present. I keep telling you. Don't let your mind wander off into the future or the past."

"I understand," said Thomas.

John then asked Thomas a question: "Where do you think Heartland is positioned on this axis? And, more important, which approach are you taking to reach your Nirvana?"

"Oh, those are good questions," Thomas responded. "I think we are still bottom left, although there are some signs of improvement. But, it's early. I guess we are following a similar approach to Mark. I need to fix the plane and fly it at the same time."

CPO Best Practices

- Build good relationships with other members of the executive team.

- Actively manage both the internal and external effectiveness of the procurement function.

- Tailor your transformation approach to the needs of your business—either "savings first," "organization first," or a balanced approach.

Interlude

U2 2742 Palma de Mallorca (PMI)—Milan Malpensa (MXP)

Cabin Attendant: What would you like, Ma'am?

Laura Braida: An orange juice and a coffee please, just black. And for my colleague here some coffee as well, I suppose.

Bernardo Mori: Oh si, si—yes, coffee would be wonderful. Is it strong? I feel like I did not sleep for a week, or I am getting older finally.

Laura Braida: Well, you do not want me to comment on your age, do you? Anyway, it hides well behind your sunglasses. But you are right, that was pretty intense, especially the evenings at the bar. But I think it was just great. I have never met any of these people before—and now they almost seem like friends. I was really surprised how big the group was!

Bernardo Mori: Oh, mamma mia.... I can see that you still have not lost your temperament and energy, even after three hangovers. Are you not exaggerating a little bit? Friends with all these people just after three days? Bella, I am trying to be your friend since one thousand days, and still you are not even looking at me ... unless you need an ally for one of your crazy strategies. But you are right—it was very good to meet all these people and to see that they are actually facing the same problems. At least this brings some consolation.

Laura Braida: Consolation? You are talking about consolation? This is a huge opportunity to really *achieve* something now! We are all in one boat, and yes, we have been facing the same challenges. However, now comes the best: Now we are all aware of this, we know each other, and can help each other out. By the way, have you met Bob from the Atlanta site? The one who is doing packaging as well?

Bernardo Mori: Bob, I think ... um, yes, sure I met him.

Laura Braida: He is a really nice guy and was totally frustrated with the number of item numbers, specs changing virtually every month, etc. He is drowning in complexity, and I thought: "Wow—finally, we are not alone with this....!" We had a very healthy discussion on this and what we could do and I feel, if I needed an opinion or any kind of help, I could call him just now [pulling her mobile phone out of her pocket].

Bernarndo Mori: Cara mia, you know that on the plane you're not allowed to....

Laura Braida: Consolation—man, you will not stop being a pessimist even if you won the Eurolottery. Actually, I do have some ideas for packaging. It will not be an easy one, but now there is top management support. I mean, did you hear what Thomas and even Ross said? I think on packaging, we can do something really big.

Bernardo Mori: Bella, you are crazy—but this is why I adore you so much.

DL 115 Barcelona (BCN)—Atlanta Hartsfield–Jackson Intl. (ATL)

Robert Donnell: By the way, talking about women, did you meet Laura from our Milan site? I think she really is great.

Carl O'Sullivan: You bet I did—had a nice chat with her at the bar.

Robert Donnell: Laura is amazing. You know how long I have been fighting against the complexity in our packaging portfolio, which is just a crazy waste of money? But no one listens, everybody has always other priorities, etc. It was like fighting against windmills, if you know what I mean. Of course you know. Anyway, Laura has been facing exactly the same issues in Italy. But she came up with some really new ideas, and she is quite convinced that with these we can tackle that whole mess. She said something about statistical methods to analyze price worthiness of certain specifications.

Carl O'Sullivan: Sounds like a lot of work to me.

Robert Donnell: It won't be easy, and it will need a lot of support from production and engineering. But for the first time ever, management seems to be interested in such things, and people really seem to listen now. I have to give Laura a buzz right away next week.

Cabin attendant: What would you like for lunch, Sir?

IB 6275 Madrid Barajas (MAD)—Chicago O'Hare Intl. (ORD)

Jason Baker: I will have the fish, please.

Amy Harmon: Don't do that. You'll be disappointed. Do you remember that wonderful barbecued fish at that lovely little place on the beach? It was the best I ever had in my life. If you eat this fish, you will be disappointed, I tell you. Actually, the whole event was just like a dream. If my husband had known about all this before, he would probably not have let me go. Not sure whether in his eyes it will still qualify as "mandatory business trip to Europe."

Cabin attendant: There you go, sir. And for you ma'am?

Amy Harmon: The pasta for me, please. Thank you.

Jason Baker: You're right. You know what is strange? It's been just three days that we were on that island. Now we are flying back and somehow it feels like weeks have passed. I still can't believe that all this has happened.

Amy Harmon: What do you mean?

Jason Baker: I mean I have been with Heartland for almost 30 years now. We have always been doing our stuff the same way. Negotiated with our preferred suppliers once or maybe twice every year, and otherwise we have been chasing orders and dealing with quality issues to keep production happy. And yes, we kept the business going.

Amy Harmon: Yes, and so?

Jason Baker: Well, now, within just three days, we learn that what we have successfully been doing all the time is suddenly not good enough anymore; that the company has a different strategy; that procurement will play a big, big role in this; that production and R&D are even officially on board? In fact, I don't even remember that you and I have ever talked longer than ten minutes with each other before, though you basically define all the products that I buy. And that now we get sent to a holiday resort in Europe to get to know each other to work better together in the future? I mean, how crazy is this?

Amy Harmon: Well, I think this is good and probably even quite a healthy development. You mean, it's all a bit too much?

Jason Baker: No, no—I think this is really fantastic! I just don't recognize my own company anymore. I cannot believe that Ross did all this— the summit, his opening speech, but I think he is damned right, man. Whether I liked him in the beginning or not, Tom from good old Autowerke is really starting to make a difference here.

TG 949 Madrid Barajas (MAD)—Bangkok Suvarnabhumi (BKK)

Prakash Chandran:	What do you think? Thomas seemed to be quite happy with the summit.
Halim Arshad:	Yes, and I think he has all the reason to be so. Things really went well at the meeting, and he seems to have a good standing with Ross also. Do you remember Ross's speech on the first day? To me it was—well, within a Heartland context I would say— groundbreaking.
Prakash Chandran:	I agree. Actually, we may have to think now what this will mean for all our future commodity strategies. Just think of palm oil, for example.
Cabin attendant:	Welcome to Bangkok and thank you for choosing Thai Airways. We wish you a pleasant stay. If you have not yet reached your final destination, we wish you a good and safe onward journey.

Chapter 24:
The Yacht Trip

The meeting ended Saturday morning, but many Heartland executives decide to stay for the weekend. John stays and charters a sailing boat for Saturday afternoon. I join him.

You should think of your team as much more like a sailing boat. At times, you have to apply the motor to push the direction, and at other times you need to let the wind take its course. It's essential that you manage that balance.

Do you see what I mean?

I think so ...

The meeting ended Saturday morning, but many Heartland executives decide to stay for the weekend. John stays and charters a sailing boat for Saturday afternoon. I join him. It had been a good meeting, but I want to have some downtime and enjoy the sea while I can—away from the corporate atmosphere.

We head out from the harbor using the engine, but once we hit the open sea there is enough wind to sail properly. The wind catches the sails, pushing the vessel through the waves. I haven't sailed very much, and I'm impressed by how much easier it is without the engine. "It's much smoother now," I shout over the spray.

"Yes, this is the way nature intended us to sail," says John. "See how she glides through the waves? Nice and delicate. Under engine power we are forcing her through; it's a much rougher trip that way."

"As long as we have some wind."

"That's true, but if we have some tailwind we should use it and not fight it. Sometimes we do need the engine to make progress, but not always. Say, isn't this a bit like what's going on at Heartland at the moment?"

I ask, "What do you mean?"

"Well, you have a vision of what you want to do. You and Ross have your feet firmly on the gas pedal pushing it through by engine power. Now and again, don't you think you ought to let the wind do some of the work for you? It may be easier and smoother."

"I'm not sure I understand the analogy," I say.

"Thomas, you can't do everything yourself. You can't drive everything from the top down by command. There is a need for some of that—people need the challenge and to improve. You don't need to push using the engine if the wind is right. But too much engine power, and the going will get rough. The boat will be too choppy in the sea and some people will fall off. Many people who fall off will be good people that you ought to keep. If you just use the engine, then I don't think things will work out."

"Are you saying I'm too pushy? You're starting to sound like Heidi." I force a laugh.

"Maybe," says John. "You're in an awful hurry to rush things along. More speed and less haste may be better for you. Like our boat—see how graceful she is under sail. Once people in your organization start to recognize that change is needed, they will drive it themselves. As a leader, you must instill the will to change, give help, guidance, and advice. But you should not micro manage everyone. You should think of your team as much more like a sailing boat. At times, you have to apply the motor to push the direction, at other times you need to let the wind take its course. It's essential that you manage that balance. Do you see what I mean?"

"I think so …" I say, not entirely convinced.

The boat continues to glide along. As the afternoon wears on, the wind starts to turn and move against us. While we make slow progress against the wind by tacking, John decides to take the sail down and use the motor.

"You see, now the wind is against us. At times, in your transformation journey, there will be moments where you need to act decisively like this. At other times, the wind needs to take its course."

I'm still confused by all these nautical analogies. I wonder, as the waves splash over the side, whether I am, indeed, trying too hard. Perhaps by pushing too much, trying to be the engine all of the time instead of letting my colleagues in Heartland use the wind, I'm part of the problem. Maybe this applies in more ways than just Heartland—an image of my fight with Heidi burns in my mind.

"Could I apply these analogies to my home life too, to marriage, to children?"

"How are things with Heidi, right now?"

"They could be better," I say. "We seem to argue a lot now, more than we used to. Actually, we never really used to argue."

"She's found the move from Germany to Fort Wayne difficult?"

"Yes, and I haven't really helped. I have been pushing too much. I pressed her to move here, and I've been so absorbed with Heartland that I haven't been listening to her. And I spend so much time away from home. I need to give Heidi more room to share her problems with me. Then, we can work them out together. Like we used to."

"Perhaps you should stop trying to drive everything in top gear—both at Heartland and at home."

"Yeah, maybe I need to think a bit more in those moments when it is better to let the wind do its work, to let the boat drift a little before trying to apply the motor again."

The boat heads toward the harbor; John navigates through the narrow channel and moors at the dock. Once the sailboat is safely tied up and we've both climbed out, John says, "Let me give you one more piece of advice, Thomas."

"Sure."

"The breakthrough will come at Heartland. People look like they are doing the right things. Keep challenging for results, but moderate that by giving praise too, and encouraging your team to keep going. Give your people the room they need to deliver. Listen to their issues, and be prepared to help them. You will get there."

He then pauses and says; "The same goes for Heidi too, I suspect."

Chapter 25:
The Horse Race

Two months have passed since the memorable strategy summit on Mallorca. In terms of Heartland Consolidated Industries, the meeting was a turning point. Procurement people clearly respect me for my vision and are following my leadership. It's even to the point where I'm looking forward to work when I wake up in the morning.

Unfortunately, I have another problem. Things at home have really turned sour. Communication with Heidi now is mostly limited to logistics—who will pick up the kids and what's for dinner. We even had a loud argument in front of the kids, something we had vowed never to do. I'm very conscious that this situation needs to change. But I also don't know what to do. My calendar is full of travel plans, which hasn't helped in fixing it either.

Most of my time is spent on status meetings with the category teams. There are a lot of things going on, and I'm really trying to follow John's advice—being 100% focused on the present. Now when I attend meetings, I don't bring any electronics. Without my iPhone I don't have to fight the temptation to check my e-mails. Between meetings, I steal a couple minutes to relax, performing some yoga poses. This helps clear my mind of distracting thoughts so I can really focus on the present. There has already been a payoff—I've managed to identify repeating patterns of problems across some category teams. By connecting people across business units and category teams, things have accelerated and there is less needless work.

Still, I feel as if time is working against me. Mallorca added to the high expectations, and soon I will have to deliver. I know Ross doesn't care about input, he just wants results—and so far all I can report is input. Others seem to share my concerns. A couple days ago, Gary Parker asked for a meeting in private.

"Thomas, I have $15 million in savings that we can claim for our global initiative. You remember that we are increasing our silo capacity for grain to be less exposed to short-term price unpredictability. We budgeted to do this with our long-term local supplier, SiloNorthern. I never liked them. They are arrogant and only average quality. So I have been working over the past twelve months to qualify a Canadian supplier, who admittedly had never done silos in the size we need. They typically work with farmers, not industry. They seem to be well connected to the Canadian steel industry, since they get much better prices than SiloNorthern. Anyway, this has materialized now. I have a green light from all involved parties and we are going to issue the purchase order for the first lot of silos today."

"Hey, thanks a lot Gary, great job!" My mind was spinning. An easy way out? If I could claim $15 million in savings now, that would take a lot of pressure off my shoulders. But then I remembered Dan Schaeffler's mantra: "Never, ever tell a lie." A lie always comes back to haunt you. "But tell me, to what extent has our global initiative helped you to realize this? This sounds like you would have had done this no matter what."

"Well, depends on the point of view. Yes, the idea has been around before all of this started. But the mindset and momentum we created with the global initiative certainly helped. We could easily make this a plausible story."

I was very pleased to hear Gary say that "we" had created the global initiative. "See Gary, this is exactly what I don't want to do. I don't want to make anything a plausible story. I just want to report rock-solid results. But I really appreciate your effort. It is great to have someone with your dedication on the team."

"Boy, you are a straight shooter! This is very different than how we played the game over here up to now. It'll take some time to get used to it. But I believe it's more fun your way in the end."

I'm taking the conversation with Gary Parker as a wake-up call. If Gary is worrying about quick wins, others will too, including Ross. So I head back to my office and cancel all meetings of secondary order for the day with the aim of developing a simple yet convincing format for updating Ross on status and progress. At Autowerke, we had had a pretty sophisticated system that I will never be able to replicate in time. And the culture here is completely different. Heartland is far more hands-on and pragmatic. After spending two hours and consuming an entire stack of yellow pad sheets, I take a break by browsing the newspaper. I've always been more into sports than politics: it's always the first section I read. The first thing I see is a picture at a local horse race. "This is it!" I yell, dropping the newspaper and going back to my yellow pad.

I draw horizontal lines, one for each of the global category teams. Next I draw vertical lines. Then I put insignias on each of the top sections. The logos stood for the common high-level process steps each team had defined. On the left I put columns for spend and savings targets; on the right I put columns for identified and for realized savings. Because this will be my key format to communicate, I produce the required electronic spreadsheet myself. At dusk, I'm finally satisfied with my result and send it to the global category leaders with this note:

Team: We need a consistent and easy to understand reporting format that allows us to communicate with our key stakeholders. Look at the attached template and let me know what you think. If you are okay with it, let's have weekly updates every Thursday by noon Fort Wayne time. Gary, would you please consolidate the input from the guys.

Thank you,
Thomas

Horse race: Template

Category	Spend (in $ mn)	Savings target (in $ mn)	Category profiled	Strategy defined	Market analyzed	Execution started	Agreements negotiated	Implementation completed	Savings (in $ mn) Identified	Implemented
Raw materials										
Packaging										
Contract manufacturing										
Logistics										
Production equipment										
Facilities and real estate										
Marketing										
General services and admin										
Total										

Two weeks later, this comes in handy. I'm standing in the parking lot with Rick Fiore, giving him advice on what new car to buy, and more specifically which engine to pick. I've become the resident expert on everything related to motor vehicles—they are still my favorite topic. I've practically talked Rick into a hybrid when Ross shows up in his old Cadillac.

"Just the two people I've been looking for! I'm looking for material for the next analyst call. Go ahead, inspire me!"

Rick gives an update on the ramp-up of the new processing plant that will propel Heartland into a completely new range of healthy products. Everything is going according to plan. Ross seems satisfied.

"So Thomas, what do you have for me?"

I've been waiting for this moment for several days now. I pull a folded printout from my breast pocket. "This is our most condensed status report. See, here are the main categories, the $60 billion of spend in scope, and the savings target of $5 billion. The little bars moving from left to right stand for the status of the categories along our process. We call this the "horse race." So you can see that seven out of ten are on plan, two are ahead of plan, and one is slightly behind plan. Overall we are making good progress and expect to deliver savings as forecasted."

"That's pretty neat. All relevant information on one page, I like it. But when are we going to see results? The analyst call would be much easier if I could throw them a bone to chew on. Is there anything I can tell them?"

Before I can open my mouth, Rick steps in. "Hey Ross, give the man a break. What Thomas has achieved in the past months is unbelievable. It feels like for the first time we really have a functioning procurement group. I can tell you, they are all over the place, and turning up the heat on my manufacturing people. I am absolutely convinced that this will deliver the results we expect."

Ross looks from one to the other and smiles. "I see, I see." He mumbles and starts toward his office.

| CPO Best Practices |

- Identify best practices where you see them in your team and challenge other teams to adopt them too.

- Be honest in the claims you make for success.

- Use simple devices to keep the CEO and other executives informed of progress.

Chapter 26:
The Breakthrough

The next day, I head in to the office early. En route, I think about my conversation with Ross yesterday. I understand I need to deliver results: Ross's patience is finite, as is Wall Street's. I'm aware that in Milan there are some negotiations that have been in play for one of the more complex packaging categories. These were with an unavoidable supplier to many of the company's plants.

I signed off on the case for negotiations a couple weeks earlier. The team is projecting strong savings. They had carried out a cost regression analysis or CRA of the many products that this supplier provides—looking at such price-sensitive variables as materials, number of folds, size, and so forth. Up to now, nobody had collected the specifications in one place globally. The team has put a huge effort into doing this over the past couple months. They collected information from 48 sites, a huge task.

The regression technique for this category had been a particular insight of the category team leader, Laura Braida. I empowered her somewhat quirky approach, sensing the strong desire to make something happen. Frankly, I had nothing to lose.

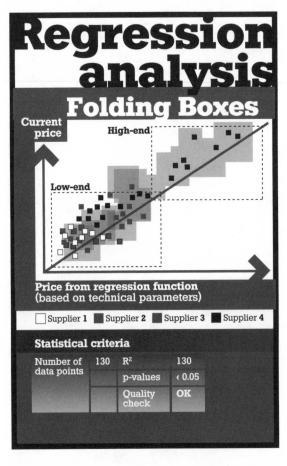

Previously each plant carried out its own separate negotiations for this category, although I doubt whether "negotiation" is the right word. By collating the specification data and analyzing it, the team has identified major discrepancies in the pricing across the products. It seems that this supplier—Coswalder Packaging—is significantly more expensive than equivalent providers to other plants. This is a major finding. No one has ever carried out this type of systematic pricing analysis at Heartland before, although it had been routine at Autowerke.

However, despite this, Coswalder is a strong source, and no one in the manufacturing sites wanted to go through the process of qualifying a different supplier. Apart from this, there is a feeling that this supplier understood their needs and supplied products that work properly in the company's packaging machines. All of these issues could be resolved if Heartland chose a different supplier, but it would take time. I don't really have time.

The analysis therefore seemed interesting, but there were serious doubts when the business case was discussed as to whether the team could pull off a major coup here quickly. I'm expecting that they will need to go through the rigmarole of a full RFP process to the marketplace before persuading the manufacturing organization to switch suppliers. My expectations of immediate results are low.

Yesterday I didn't check on the progress—I didn't expect experienced supply-side negotiators to reduce the price immediately during the meeting. I did see a cryptic e-mail from Laura: "Thomas, the negotiations went fine today. We asked the other side to make a revised offer by 10 a.m. CET [Central European Time] tomorrow. Regards, Laura."

I had no idea what that means, and I haven't worried about it. Personally, a deadline that quick I find a little unwise. But rather than stress about it, I've left it to Laura and her team—they know what they're doing. I grab a coffee downstairs and head up to my office. While in the elevator, i check my iPhone.

I almost spit out my coffee when I read Laura's newest e-mail. "Thomas, we have carried out an initial analysis of the revised offer from Coswalder. Still need to finalize the numbers, but our first impression is that it will equate to savings of $28 million over 12 months. It's a bit early to share this more widely, but we wanted you to know. Regards, Laura."

This is way beyond my expectations—at least immediately. I bound down the corridor to my office, shut the door, and immediately dial Laura's number. The phone rings. I get voice mail. Trying to sound calm, I leave a simple message: "Laura, Thomas. I just got your e-mail, sounds good. Give me a call when you have a moment."

I turn on my computer and look at my schedule for the day. The phone rings. It's Laura: "Thomas, you called."

"Yes, sounds like you guys had a good day yesterday. Have I understood your e-mail properly—$28 million in savings?"

"That's right."

"Are you sure?"

"We had to do some checking but we've done that now. We're comfortable that it is correct."

"Gee, what sort of negotiation did you guys do down there?"

"Well," Laura says, "we did as we agreed. We provided Coswalder with the data analysis in advance of the meeting so that they would not be able to claim they needed time to react. As you saw, it was quite shocking. They did try to rationalize it in the meeting, but that didn't really work."

"I see. How did our manufacturing guys do?"

"They were excellent. We held the internal alignment calls that we had talked about, to ensure that everybody on the team bought into our negotiation goals and strategy. We then did the half-day internal workshop with us all face-to-face the day before the negotiations to develop strong messages and align our choreography. Also, we projected Coswalder's potential reactions in the negotiation and already crafted our responses to those. The manufacturing guys got quite worked up about the price differences. Our site director here, Luigi, was particularly upset about Coswalder not playing fairly. He gave the critical messages yesterday to them that we are quite prepared to go through the pain of changing suppliers if we have to."

"Sounds good," I say.

"Yes, the role of manufacturing was critical. The call that Steve Rider, the Global VP, made to Coswalder's CEO before the negotiation was also very helpful. In the past, Coswalder has been very good at making sure everyone from manufacturing is on their side. They have made sure that all real negotiations are just at plant level. In the past, anything at the global level has rarely been more than a relationship-building conversation. We have never had the data or the internal commitment to do anything else before. This is different, and Coswalder realized that too."

"We need to make sure that we capture these success factors for the other teams," I say. "Well done."

"Thank you," says Laura.

"By the way, how public is this now? Who else knows?"

"Luigi and his guys know, of course."

"We need a formal communication, Laura," I say. "It would be good to ensure we communicate the message properly."

I see Ross walking toward my office. "Oh," I say. "Ross is just coming in to ask about something. I'll call you back."

Ross enters the office. "Have you seen the news from Milan?"

"You mean the Coswalder deal?" said Thomas.

"Yes."

"You found out fast, Ross. I only just heard myself."

"I didn't get to be head of this business without knowing what is going on," replies Ross. "It isn't only bad news that travels fast around here. Your team did a good job there. Well done."

"Thank you."

"What is that price assessment technique that they used there in Milan?"

"CRA," I say. "They basically run regressions on the product variables and compare these to the impact on price. This is then used to identify discrepancies to help us negotiate."

"It must be good if it gets us these results. Get that category manager of yours over there ... Laura?"

"Yes, Laura Braida."

"Yes, get her to explain that approach to me some time." Ross then says, "We'll expect the same level of results everywhere else now." He pauses for a moment.

"No, that's wrong. We'll expect more results—as the team gets better." He winks and smiles, walking back down the corridor. "Be sure to set that briefing up."

CPO Best Practices

- Pricing analyses can be very powerful levers in a negotiation—data really is power.

- An aligned and empowered negotiating team that includes procurement and people from the function needing goods or services is crucial when negotiating with external suppliers.

- Selected messaging by top level executives to suppliers in support of the negotiating team can be valuable.

Chapter 27:
Laura Achieves "Guru" Status

I really appreciate the opportunities you and Ross are giving me.

By sending Laura around, I've been relieved of a lot of travel and can spend more time at home.

I enjoy having Laura around and have tentatively started to talk her into moving here permanently. Ross agrees.

Getting Laura to Fort Wayne is proving to be easy. After talking to Ross, I immediately called her back to share the feedback. Laura is clearly gung-ho when it comes to managing her own career. With my tacit green light, and after I checked with Helen, she agreed to a meeting with Ross for next Monday morning. She happily spent Sunday on the plane. She, Ross, and I then spent all of Monday morning together.

Ross was eager to understand the mechanics involved in CRA. He kept repeating what he learned to Laura, who turned out to be a gifted tutor. I'm sure that as much as Ross was genuinely interested in understanding CRA, he was already rehearsing the next analyst call. There was a certain sparkle in Ross's eyes about breaking the good news to the market.

A little before noon, Ross left for the airport. "I'm sorry for not being able to take you out for lunch to celebrate," Ross said, "but I'm sure Thomas will take care of that. And while you are talking, why don't you discuss how this success can be rolled out to other categories."

That was six weeks ago. A lot has happened since then. Savings have jumped slightly past $100 million and are now coming from several categories. Remarkably, Laura's teams have delivered about 80 percent of these savings. While CRA is the method of choice for packaging, she has gone down an entirely different route for flavors. Her team contracts the food science lab of Milan University to break down the components of high volume flavors at Heartland's main sites. They are able to prove that across all products, Heartland is essentially paying for filler and the same basic materials. Differences in taste and smell are accounted for by tiny nuances in composition, which does not at all explain the huge price differences. When Laura threatens to share these insights with peers in the food industry, the key supplier—a French multinational—gives in.

Despite Laura's quick rise to guru status at Heartland Consolidated Industries, I don't feel jealous. I'm proud to have her on our team. Encouraged by Ross, I start to pull Laura out of operational work to put her into more of a program management role. She is now on most of the regular review meetings with other category teams as well and proves to be a great source of unconventional ideas on how to tackle hairy problems. In the majority of cases, her advice has proven to be spot-on.

By sending Laura around, I've been relieved of a lot of travel. Laura doesn't seem to mind the heavy load of travel. In one of our relatively seldom private conversations, she told me how lucky she feels in her new role. "You know Thomas, most of my peers from university struggle to gain a foothold in professional life. Getting research or a teaching position at the university is very hard considering the budget cuts everywhere. And industry normally doesn't know what to do with mathematicians. The smartest graduate from my class still lives at his parents' house because he can't find a job to pay his rent. I really appreciate the opportunities you and Ross are giving me."

Laura's eagerness to travel gives me more time at home. Whenever possible, I pick up the kids, check their homework, and prepare dinner. But despite my best efforts, my relationship with Heidi still remains on the rocky side. Communication is still down to a minimum, but at least we haven't had any arguments lately.

In her new capacity, Laura comes to Fort Wayne every other week. I enjoy having her around and have tentatively started to talk her into moving here permanently. Ross agrees.

The reason for this particular visit to Fort Wayne is special. Ross has decided to focus the annual Heartland spring party on the procurement initiative. Laura's team will be singled out as exemplary, and all of them are clearly excited about meeting Ross on stage. When I learn that the spring party is meant to include spouses, I initially hesitate to ask Heidi, for fear of being rejected. Surprisingly, she agrees immediately. "Sure, I'll come. There aren't too many things going on in Fort Wayne. It will be nice to dress up and go out as we used to do." One of the neighbor's daughters, a sophomore in high school, is recruited to look after the kids, as she has done several times before.

CPO Best Practices

- Replicate success around the organization.

- Recognize and reward talent wherever you find it.

- Hold regular and open reviews of content across the teams.

Chapter 28:
Annual Heartland Consolidated Industries Spring Party

Chapter 28 | Annual Heartland Consolidated Industries Spring Party

As tradition prescribes, the spring party is held at the Fort Wayne convention center, the only place big enough to seat such a large number of people.

Inside, it's clear that the organizing committee has done a marvelous job. There are cocktail tables interspaced by lounge areas but no fixed seating. This gives guests the opportunity to float around and talk to many different people during the evening. Waiters are offering appetizers and drinks. I shake a lot of hands and introduce Heidi to a lot of people. She seems bewildered.

At eight, Ross delivers a warm, punchy, short speech. He makes a big show of introducing the procurement initiative and singles out Laura and her category team for the early success with the CRA. A video is shown with short personal messages from many of the contributors to the procurement initiative, including me and Laura. At the end of the video, Ross asks all the contributors to the procurement initiative present to come on stage so that they can get a round of applause.

I look down from the stage just in time to see Heidi heading toward the exit with all her things. Bewildered, I step off the stage and follow her.

Eventually, I find her sitting in the car.

"Honey, what's wrong? I have been looking for you all over the place."

"Are you having an affair?"

"I beg your pardon? What are you talking about?"

"I was standing next to two men who said 'everybody knows' you and that Italian woman are having an affair."

"Laura? That's ridiculous! We're working together, that's all."

"Thomas Sutter, I am asking you again. Are you having an affair?"

"Christ, what rubbish! She is just a colleague, albeit a very good one. She's saved the day for the procurement initiative and she is very dedicated and smart. But an affair? How can you believe all this nonsense people are talking about—don't you trust me?"

"Thomas, you are not giving me a straight answer. I'm asking you one last time. Are you having an affair?"

"I am not having an affair. I've never ever accused you of having an affair. And if I remember correctly, most of your colleagues are male. For a change, I have a female colleague for the first time I can remember and get accused of having an affair. We aren't even discussing this in a decent way. You walk out on me and make me look like an idiot in front of my colleagues."

Heidi seems satisfied with the answer, yet she is shaken. We decide just to go home. We drive home in silence, but I can't help but notice that she is crying. Can things get much worse between us?

Chapter 29:
Just Virtual Savings?

The boardroom is booked and on Friday morning we have our meeting with Ross, Garner (CFO), Rick (Production), Hernando (R&D), and Scarlet (Marketing) on-site while being connected via video-conference with the site managers from the major locations in Europe, Africa, and the Middle and Far East.

Time flies. We have been working on the program now for six months and have made great progress. While Laura and I carefully manage frequent communication to all stakeholders, we decide it would be a good idea to have a more formal committee too. This will create reports about our first successes in more detail, and align our strategic plans for the upcoming weeks and months.

I help Laura compile the deck. Her first draft is good but a little too "mathematical." Being fact based is one thing, but I've explained that we need to win both the hearts and minds of the audience. The boardroom is booked and on Friday morning, we have our meeting with Ross, Garner (CFO), Rick (Production), Hernando (R&D), and Scarlet (Marketing) on-site while being connected via videoconference with the site managers from the major locations in Europe, Africa, and the Middle and Far East.

I make a quick introduction about the Go for Gold initiative and where things stand, and then hand it over to Laura, allowing her to present the results accomplished already.

Horse race: Good intermediary results

Category	Spend (in $ mn)	Savings target (in $ mn)	Category profiled	Strategy defined	Market analyzed	Execution started	Agreements negotiated	Implementation completed	Savings (in $ mn) Identified	Savings (in $ mn) Implemented
Raw materials	31,200	1,240							1,130	599
Packaging	4,800	720							842	233
Contract manufacturing	6,050	900							770	83
Logistics	4,200	630							693	427
Production equipment	2,420	360							638	96
Facilities and real estate	2,360	200							170	9
Marketing	5,950	650							470	12
General services and admin	3,070	300							244	47
Total	**60,050**	**5,000**							**4,957**	**1,506**

When Laura presents the $5 billion in identified savings, Garner asked a question that likely many of the site managers are asking themselves: "Laura, this chart is nice. However, when I look into our books, I hardly see any of the savings you are talking about. Are these 'PowerPoint' savings only?"

I step in immediately. This question doesn't come as much of a surprise. "Garner, I'm glad you asked. It is actually part of the reason we wanted to have this meeting, so everyone understands what the different numbers mean. In our chart, you will see that we distinguish between 'identified' and 'implemented' savings. These are two out of five levels of "hardness in savings" we are distinguishing to provide you with concrete and reliable figures. Let me quickly show a corresponding slide from the appendix:"

Program Management Office		
Hardness of Savings		
All savings potentials are evaluated based on "hardness of savings."		
Degree of Hardness	**Type**	**Comment**
1	Savings Potential	Analytical indication that product/service could be published at a lower price.
2	Quoted Savings	Credible supplier offers same or comparable product/service at a lower price.
3	Recommended Savings	Validity of lower prices confirmed in negotiations (and by supplier visits).
4	Contracted Savings	Product/service validated and ready to be introduced. Deal closed with supplier.
5	Realized Savings	Product/service at lower price demonstrates reliable performance in value-adding process.

I continue. "We do have some savings in packaging, where new contracts are signed, and even some leveraged-back savings have been agreed to. For initiatives still in Step 1, 2, 3, or 4, the savings are 'savings potential.' The further along we are in the process, the more understanding we have about our spend, our requirements, the market (including benchmarks), and the levers we are planning to apply—and so the more confident we are about the savings potential. During the actual negotiations, we collect actual market pricing and can calculate savings for several scenarios based on supplier quotations. These are 'quoted savings.' The quotation that we finally accept is classified as 'recommended savings'—then that final quotation still needs 'ink on the paper' to become 'contracted savings.' 'Realized savings' come in once we order goods and services under the new contracts, and therefore it will take some time before they are in the books. In all cases the savings are measured against a price and cost baseline that is agreed up front at the start of the work. Laura is tracking the savings in detail, plus estimated percentage EBIT [earnings before interest and taxes] realization over the next 24 months in a corresponding SharePoint database. Shall we have a separate session early next week so we can provide some further explanations?"

Garner is satisfied with my explanation and so we continue with the "category deep dives" we'd prepared. Laura asks the category heads for logistics and packaging to each provide a 30-minute presentation. Fred Jensan from logistics goes first. Fred is proud to have a chance to talk about his category in front of top management for the first time in his long career here, and he explains how "collaborative optimization" is the fundamental leap we've made so far.

Garner quizzes Fred on exactly what this concept means. Fred proudly explains the approach. In a traditional situation, the supplier offers are constrained to a particular approach specified by the customer. For a category such as logistics, where there is potentially a vast range of different routings and options, this artificiality constrains suppliers to make offers that are not aligned to their optimal cost structure.

In contrast, under the "collaborative optimization" approach, the Heartland logistics RFPs did not include fixed specifications of the precise routes and transshipment requirements. Instead, the tender specified Heartland's needs and allowed potential suppliers to identify the appropriate logistics options to meet the need. This enabled the suppliers to make the precise offers that were most closely aligned to their own optimal cost structures and existing networks. Effectively, the suppliers quoted scenarios. By using advanced analytical techniques, Heartland was then able to compare the scenarios on a like basis and establish which precise pattern of supplier scenarios was most beneficial. This resulted in a mixed award decision in which different suppliers were responsible for different discrete parts of the overall requirement.

Garner quickly understands the power of this approach. He muses that it could perhaps be applied to other categories where supplier-award scenarios can vary and where there are a large number of specifications. The team pointed out that the approach was accordingly already being applied for packaging and being considered for contract labor.

The meeting closes, having gone very well, with a constructive dialogue. I feel that the key to this has been threefold. First, we were prepared and did not have to think up answers too much "on the spot." Second, we have been open in addressing questions and challenges. Third, we have steered the right balance in explaining enough of the technical content so that the audience could buy into it while keeping the discussion at the right level for senior executives.

CPO Best Practices

- Make savings realization transparent within active management of the different "stages."

- Content and fact-based deep dives are good vehicles for obtaining buy-in to the actual solutions that are being proposed, as well as a way of obtaining wider input.

- Advance preparation for program meetings pays dividends!

Chapter 30:
It Is Not Just
About Savings

I walk into the elevator with Scarlet. "I thought that was a good session," she says. "I just wanted to talk to you about some of the work your people are doing with my marketing teams in Europe."

"Do you mean the point-of-sale material initiative?"

"Yes, I am pleased with what has happened so far. The team is genuinely thinking about how the overall service will be improved, and not just about savings. You know this is crucial so that our products are properly marketed in the stores. I have never seen procurement think about this before. Usually, they just want to nickel and dime the contracts with the vendors that my people have chosen. This is much more strategic."

The background to this was that we had set up a cross-functional team to look at the point-of-sale category in Germany and Austria. Scarlet had been quite resistant to this initially. She had questioned whether more procurement involvement would help. My idea had actually been to look at all of the marketing spend rather than just point of sale. I really wanted to address point of sale fully across all of our regions, not just in a few countries. Owing to Scarlet's concerns, I had compromised and persuaded her to agree to the pilot approach. Not ideal, but at least it got something happening.

I asked Hans Huttisch—the Austrian who had said so much in the Fort Wayne conference that went so poorly—to lead the initiative from procurement. His English language skills would be less critical for a pilot focused in this geography. Additionally, I had gotten to know him a little more and had understood that he was very keen to upgrade the role of procurement. His purely country-focused position in Austria frustrated him, and he saw great personal opportunity to work on a more global basis and make a difference. The point-of-sale pilot was partly a way to test this.

However, I had taken a calculated risk. The success of the pilot was the key to enable us to drive results elsewhere in the point-of-sale category. It was also crucial for earning Scarlet's trust so that we could play a more proactive role in other marketing spend areas. My instinct was that we needed to take a more active approach with the global advertising agency, for example. Unless we succeeded here, we would not be able to do this. We needed to earn Scarlet's trust.

To manage the risk, or at least to ensure that I had early warning of any problems, I had asked for weekly conference call updates with Hans. As a result, I felt pretty close to the work. Hans had set to it with gusto. The team included a couple of representatives from marketing as well as from our supply-chain organization. They looked at the end-to-end process for producing point-of-sale material rather than just the existing contracts and commercial relationships. Over time, it was clear that things were progressing. Accordingly, I was able to shorten the updates and move them to biweekly. This also gave Hans the message that I trusted his work.

Key findings from the initial analysis were that there is no end-to-end accountability for ensuring that material is delivered to stores on time to support promotional activity. There are also a number of poorly managed handoffs between the producers of the material and the distributors, which contribute to the problems. Material is not even dispatched to stores in a format that can be easily managed on-site either. This creates complexity for our trade customers and does not give them an incentive to maximize impact for us with consumers. Furthermore, different specifications and printed words are used even between Germany and Austria. Given the common language, this makes absolutely no sense, and has no justification. The upshot of all this is that we have far too many variations of material to manage, the material arrives late in stores, and is not fit for purpose when it does arrive.

The team's recommendation has been to select one end-to-end supplier that will take responsibility for the supply chain, with agreed and monitored service-level agreements. Additionally, internal governance will be put in place to ensure that there are controls on agreeing to new variations of the materials. The marketing function has bought into this recommendation. What tipped the balance was the positive impact on service levels. Clearly, marketing valued the savings, but this would not have been enough to get support. Scarlet has now also asked that the scope be widened to be pan-European rather than just focused on Germany and Austria. The initial commercial offers have been received now from three potential vendors who could meet our requirements. Already we think there is a benefit potential of 12% on the current cost. The final contract will include incentives for meeting the service-level requirements—both penalties for falling short and rewards for exceeding them.

There is still a lot of work to do, and we will need to manage the implementation, as well as the ongoing vendor performance once we have completed the selection. Nevertheless, this is a real breakthrough, and Scarlet clearly seemed happy from our conversation.

As we leave the elevator, she says, "Thomas, I'll ask Jane to set up a meeting if that is OK with you. I'd like to understand how you can help us deal with the agency. We're having some issues. I'd appreciate your thoughts."

"I'd be happy to talk," I say.

CPO Best Practices

- Do not only focus on price and external cost—service levels, quality, and supplier innovation are often crucial.

- Be pragmatic in what you ask stakeholders to agree to at the start—recognize that trust has to be earned.

- Manage your personal involvement in initiatives according to impact and risk—but also recognize the consequences for team motivation of higher and lower levels of personal intervention.

- Ensure that implementation and ongoing vendor management issues are always considered in supplier selection decisions—this is crucial to avoid benefit leakage.

Chapter 31:
Gearing Up

I enter Ross's office for a quick meeting he'd arranged on short notice. I wonder what's up.

"Hi Tom. Please come in. Take a seat."

"Good morning Ross," I say. "How are things? How did the analyst conference go yesterday?"

"Poorly. This is exactly why I called you in. One of those analysts almost drove me mad, kept asking for our productivity in procurement, and how it compares with that of our competitors, etc. He almost started a lecture about some supposedly new procurement KPI [key performance indicators]. I never liked analysts that much anyway, but this guy really was a pain. So, what is your view about our productivity in procurement?"

I pause, wondering where to begin.

"Well, there are many procurement key performance indicators out there. Regarding productivity, well, at Autowerke we used to look at it for individual sourcing initiatives on a high level, tracking expected benefits versus total labor days invested. At Heartland, however, we aren't fully there yet. I mean, we are in the process of building our new procurement organization, producing savings in parallel, at the same time. And you know there are already some amazing success stories. Once we start cashing in on them, we will keep track of those savings, of course."

I could tell Ross had a point and was going to make it. He tells me he supports me 100% and will continue to do so. He adds that he knows the savings will fall to the bottom line at some point. Then he looks at me closely and says, "But on this one I need an answer from you before the next conference. Otherwise, those guys will keep haunting me and all the value we create from procurement will go down the drain with our share price. This is all about communication, Thomas. So, give me a good story about how we steer Heartland's financial procurement performance—and not about labor days invested into one lighthouse initiative. Let me know if you need any support."

"I understand. I will involve Laura. As you know, she is very creative and her math background will be more than helpful. Also, I will need someone from finance. Carlos, the head of finance and controlling would be ideal.

Ross says, "Done. Anything else?"

"Who should we talk to about getting the final KPI endorsed? You, obviously, and who else?"

"Whatever you decide with our dear CFO Garner will be fine with me. Good luck. I'm counting on you."

He turns back toward his desk, and I leave the office, thinking about getting the team together for a meeting. I'm also thinking that rather than call it a KPI, it'd be more effective, and easier to relate to others, if it were called something like a "procurement performance management" metric.

Within a week, I have Carlos and Laura, who has come to Fort Wayne, sitting in my office. I begin by explaining why Ross gave us this challenge.

"I have done some research in the meantime and indeed, there is a brand new KPI that is being implemented at many companies now. Analysts seem to like it quite a lot and to be honest, it does seem interesting.

Carlos says, "Tell us more."

"It is a productivity measure for procurement organizations that focuses purely on 'hard' financial benefits. It's a ratio with total procurement costs in the denominator. You track it on a period-by-period basis. It can be aggregated from team level, to country level, to group level. The purpose is to look at procurement from a finance perspective."

I walk over to the whiteboard, where I begin writing downs some figures.

"For example, Laura, you and your team have generated approximately $80 million in annualized savings. Let's assume half of this, roughly $40 million, will hit the bottom line this year. What is the annual cost of your procurement teams over there?

"About $3 million," she answers without a blink.

I say, "Including rent, other infrastructure, bought-in services, and everything?

"Well, then let's say $4 million.

"OK," I continue, "then the KPI—your procurement performance management ratio—would be $40 million in financial benefits over $4 million procurement cost, so a ten to one return. Not bad at all!

Carlos has been listening closely. "Obviously, we need to know some more detail about it, but so far it sounds OK to me. So, what is the issue with it?"

Before I can say anything, Laura jumps in. "Well, the issue is, as always, where does the data come from and how can it be made consistent? So we need a procedure. The input has to come from the teams on a regular basis. We need to give them a tool that must be easy to use—probably some kind of data-entry mask on an intranet site. With that we can ensure that data is entered all in the same format and structure, so there are no inconsistencies from that end. But then of course everybody still needs to fill in the same kind of data. That means we need to be damned clear about the underlying definitions. That's not going to be easy. Do you have the exact definition of that KPI, Thomas?

I nod. "We still need to fine-tune it a bit, but in principle: yes. The logic is quite cool: If you had just one aggregated figure, you couldn't do very much with it other than comparing yourself with other companies. But in fact, the KPI breaks it down into the different drivers of financial procurement performance."

I draw a diagram on the board that shows what I call value-creation drivers, like spend coverage, yield, savings percentage, etc., on one side, and cost drivers like personnel, infrastructure, and so forth on the other. I tell them that numbers are collected on that level, so it gets quite tangible for the people who have to provide it. And I add that management can see exactly which drivers are either boosting or destroying current productivity levels, making it pretty clear what needs to be fixed next.

Laura is clearly impressed. She says, "Wow. This means if we manage to roll this out we would have a regular productivity benchmark, plus a kind of road map indicating the next improvement steps? It sounds great! But …"

"What?" I ask, seeing her tense up.

"It will be a tough piece of work to get this up and running before the next analyst conference. And let's face it—not doing it will not be an option anyway, will it? Carlos?"

"Sounds like we have plan," Carlos says. "Let's think it through a bit more and then have a conversation with Garner.

Carlos, Laura, and I spend the next two days hammering out the details of the KPI and how it will be rolled out to the rest of the procurement organization at Heartland. We're now going to Garner's office to show him the results of our work, and hopefully OK it.

We wait for a few minutes outside his office, then Garner opens the door and motions us in. "Hi all. Sorry for making you wait. Please come in, take a seat. So, tell me about our "procurement productivity management"—I got that right, didn't I?"

"Yes," I say. "I know you were in on the last analyst call where we got pounded for not having the latest procurement KPI. As you know, Ross charged Laura, Carlos, and I to put our heads together to develop a bulletproof and pragmatic concept to track and report—and to steer—the productivity of our new procurement function. We would like to introduce this concept to you and, provided you feel comfortable with it, roll it out as soon as possible to be prepared in time for the next conference.

Garner smiled and said, "Well, you know, I've been around quite a bit in my professional life, and none of the procurement heads of any of the companies I worked for were ever able to show me where to find all their great savings in the EBIT. And now, you guys have discovered the silver bullet—well, actually the bulletproof concept for it? With all due respect for the many recent achievements in our procurement…." He winked, to show us he would listen with an open mind. "Carlos, what do you think of this?"

"Actually, Garner, I think that we have achieved a breakthrough here. This could really become a great tool for managing our procurement performance internally—and for handling the analysts. It'll keep them happy on the next conference call at any rate. If I didn't believe this, I—well, we all—would not be sitting here now.

Garner shifted in his chair. "OK, seems as if you were all pretty convinced about your new concept. I want to hear all about it. But what is different now? Why does this relate directly to our profit-and-loss [P&L] statement and all the other reports I have seen from other procurement chiefs didn't?"

Once again, Laura is quick with the answer: "Because our productivity measure is purposefully designed to match your own view of finance, and the definitions are quite strict. We also apply a strict period view of the benefits—spillovers into next year will be accounted for in the next year, and spillovers from last year will be shown this year. Then we track only hard financial benefits that can be found in our books."

Laura continues to explain that procurement will apply a very comprehensive, total cost-of-ownership view. This means if we buy a new packaging film with better specs, even at a higher unit price, but manage by this to increase throughput on our production line, generating net cost savings on our finished goods, this will be considered as a value contribution as well. So, we are talking about way more than just price. And on the cost side also, we cover everything—costs of staff, infrastructure, training, etc.—in a period form. So, in summary, I think this gets us as close as can be to our P&L."

Garner says, "Sounds quite reasonable. And you, Carlos, you buy into this?"

"Yes, sir. And I believe the analysts will, too."

Garner laughs and says, "So, if this is all so easy and obvious, what the hell is all that magic about that people always associate with procurement numbers?"

"Well," I say, "probably issues around data transparency, alignment, etc. But let's not dwell on this. The nice thing about our KPI is that it breaks down procurement's value contribution into tangible drivers. Let me define these for you." I write down the following on my legal pad while saying them out loud:

Spend coverage: The amount of spend that procurement addresses.

Yield: The savings achieved on the spend that procurement tackles.

Velocity: The actual number of times that procurement addresses a category. "Of course, all the savings in the world are only delivered if the deals are actually applied." I return to the legal pad and continue to write.

Compliance: The extent to which our supplier deals are used.

I rip off the page and hand it to Garner.

"The basic logic around compliance is that you can only generate value from spend that you control. In other words, you need to cover it, and then actually address it, through sourcing initiatives. The total amount of savings is obviously driven by the savings percentage achieved on the addressed spend—

the yield. But you will never find it in the bottom line if people do not buy from the new contracts, meaning if compliance is poor."

"Well," says Garner, "I have never looked at procurement this way, I have to admit."

I continue. "And now imagine there is an issue with spend coverage—it is, say, only 40%. First of all, this means that there is a huge blind spot, big potential for productivity improvement. But then of course the next question will be why this is so. Is it because the spend is not visible? Then we need to talk about data transparency. Or is it visible, but procurement does not have the mandate to manage it? Then we may have to discuss governance. Or is all this given but still coverage is low? Then, maybe, procurement needs to be more proactive and improve its stakeholder management."

I see that I have Garner's complete attention—I think he is coming around. "Finally," I say, "and this is probably the most important point—this insight will help us to steer procurement's work in a much more proactive, forward-looking way. It will help us to manage procurement in a very focused and transparent way. We have never had anything like that.

"Put it this way," adds Carlos, "with this, we can now build an appealing story around procurement performance rather than simply react to questions. Just have a look at this simple example—it could be from one of our local units overseas:

	Today	After Improvement
Total Spend	$2.8 Billion	$2.74 Billion
Spend Covered	86%	86%
Spend Sourced	77%	77%
Yields	2.6%	4.0%
Compliance	68%	80%
Processing Costs	$10.7 Million	$10.7 Million
Productivity	3.1	5.4
Financial Results Delivered	$33 Million	$58 Million

"If we roll this concept out in Heartland," Carlos says, "we can not only claim that our procurement performance is crystal clear and transparent, we can even make a proactive statement that from now on we have all the means to systematically manage procurement by its financial performance, on an individual driver level—and that we will do so."

Garner stands up. "You've got me. As far as I am concerned, go ahead and implement. Thanks Laura, thanks gentlemen."

―――――――――――――

Garner writes a short note to Ross:

Ross,

Thomas and his folks just showed their concept of procurement performance management to me. It's good. I've told them that I am fine with rolling it out.

Best,

Garner

P.S. Just in case you can't make the next analyst conference—happy to step in for you.

| CPO Best Practices |

- Actively track and manage the overall return on investment that the procurement function is delivering. Introduce a performance culture.

- Decompose and manage the key drivers of benefit—"spend coverage," "velocity," "yield," and "compliance."

- Do not only focus on "savings"—manage the other sources of procurement value including quality and risk mitigation.

Chapter 32:
Launching the New Procurement Organization

etailed roles and responsibilities need to be describe
n a RASIC format for core Procurement processes

Procurement RASIC		Board	CPO	Central Experts	Commodity manag
Strategic Purchasing	Category profiling			A	S
	Category strategy development			A	S
	Supply market analysis				R
	Supplier selection				

Today, I called for a meeting to formally agree on the new organization of procurement.

Operational Purchasing	Demand aggregation
	Contract management
	Allocation planning
	Order management
	Transaction management
	Supplier performance measurement
	Corrective actions

e decision, **A**uthority to decide, Supp

It is important to notice, the results we see so far have been achieved through a new way of working.

There is one person on the procurement team who has demonstrated early on what can be achieved at Heartland. Let's give Laura a big hand!

Summer is nearly over. Driving to the office, I reflect on the last couple of months. A lot has happened. I'm pleased by the turnaround I've managed in procurement. What seemed like a disaster has become one of my greatest professional successes so far. Unfortunately, I can't say the same for my home life. Despite many attempts from my side—and if I'm honest, attempts from Heidi's side—we have grown even further apart. Any innocent conversation between us has the potential to turn into a bitter argument. And in every argument things are said that add to the heavy burden our relationship has to carry. I'm not entirely sure about Heidi's status in her law firm. Judging from the time she's spent working late at night and the determination with which she leaves the house in the morning, things seem to look better.

Making the best of the situation, I'm trying to spend quality time with the kids and focusing most of my energy on the job. With cost savings piling up and the financial function convinced with the help of our procurement performance management concept, I feel ready to take things to the next level. I've spent the past few weeks working on an organizational concept that is inspired by what I've seen at Autowerke and will be revolutionary at Heartland Consolidated Industries. I've gotten smarter since my failures in the spring, and I've rallied a lot of key people at Heartland for support. I started with Rick, who surprisingly I now consider a friend. Although Rick was initially skeptical, he's finally signaled his support. I've gone through his key reports in manufacturing and engineering and through my own procurement team.

I've also pre-sold the idea to Ross. Rather than asking for a formal meeting and walking Ross through a couple of well-prepared slides, I've learned to stroll by Ross's office to see if his door is open. Ideas are best discussed with Ross informally over coffee. Ross has an incredible memory and a sharp intellect. He asks a couple of questions that usually open a fresh perspective on a problem and give hints on how to get things done at Heartland. Once this type of meeting is done, Ross is happy to receive reports about what has been decided between the executives.

Today, I called for a meeting to formally agree on the new organization of procurement. I've arranged the meeting around the monthly review of the procurement initiative that brought all procurement leaders to Fort Wayne anyway. In parallel, Rick has invited the key manufacturing and engineering leaders.

I start the meeting with a recap of the journey procurement at Heartland has taken so far and give an overview of the savings in the pipeline.

"It is important to notice that the results we see so far have been achieved through a new way of working. We changed three things. First, and most important, we have instilled pride in procurement. People feel part of a mission and that they are being taken very seriously by top management.

"Second, we work across organizational silos. Within procurement, we leverage Heartland's size. Before, Heartland used to buy like many individual medium-sized enterprises. Now we buy like the global consumer goods giant we are. But this holds true when we look at cross-functional collaboration as well. Whatever we do, we bring in our cousins from manufacturing and engineering and they involve us early on as well.

"Third, we work with new differentiated approaches. Procurement does not work with a 'one size fits all mindset.' For us, strategizing always starts with comparing our demand power with the power of our suppliers. Depending on that balance of power, we either impose target prices, or collaborate, or do other appropriate things."

I pause, drink some coffee, and observe the participants of the meeting. There are many friendly faces, and most of them are nodding. "Now over the past weeks, I've had conversations with most of you on how to make our achievements sustainable and to take things to the next level. The downside of the current state of affairs is that it is all project based. There is a risk that once the projects are over and the initial excitement about savings cools down, things might fall back to what they used to be.

"This is why I propose that we agree on a new organizational model in procurement that makes the changes permanent. The key element of this new model is a matrix. The vertical dimension of this matrix is basically the procurement activities that Heartland always had. It is division, business unit, and site oriented. The key task of this type of procurement is to keep our plants running and ensure that we have the right quality and quantity of product available at the right time and at the right price. I call this type of procurement 'operational procurement.'

"The horizontal dimension of the matrix is what we have introduced with the procurement initiative. It looks across divisions, business units, and sites and tries to leverage Heartland's size. All of you know that this means much more than volume bundling. There's only a very limited number of suppliers that can serve us around the globe. But for most of our categories, an approach that works in one site will also work for another site, even on a different continent and with a totally different supplier. We want to have category experts to apply state-of-the-art approaches across all of Heartland rather than reinvent the wheel locally. I call this type of procurement 'strategic procurement.'"

Detailed roles and responsibilities need to be described in a RASIC format for core procurement processes

Procurement RASIC		Board	CPO	Central experts	Commodity manager	Local site buyer	Local site purchasing mgr.
Strategic Purchasing	Category profiling		A	S	R	S	S
	Category strategy development		A	S	R	S	S
	Supply market analysis			R	A	S	S
	Supplier selection and negotiation			S	A	S	S
	Implementation			S	A	S	S
Operational Purchasing	Demand aggregation			S	A	S	S
	Contract management			S	A	S	A
	Allocation planning				S	R	A
	Order management				S	R	A
	Transaction management				S	R	A
	Supplier performance measurement		A	S	R	S	S
	Corrective actions			S	R	S	A

Responsibility to prepare decision, **A**uthority to decide, **S**upport preparation, **I**nformed after decision, **C**onsulted during preparation

"The interaction between strategic procurement and operational procurement is clear. Strategic procurement sets the guidelines, and operational procurement operates within these guidelines. In extreme cases, this may mean that a local site will have to swallow a slightly higher price if it benefits the group overall."

"We will not introduce this new model overnight. We expect leaders of the horizontal dimension—we call them global category officers—to emerge in the procurement initiative. In total, we will have eight global category officers. With the seven division procurement directors, they will be my direct reports. Together, the 16 of us will manage procurement at Heartland. We expect to complete staffing by the end of next year, but we will start with the first nomination for category officer with the introduction of this new organizational model. There is one person in the procurement team who has demonstrated early on what can be achieved at Heartland. I know I have your unanimous support for nominating Laura Braida as Heartland's first global category officer. Let's give Laura a hand!"

Considering that there are only 40 people in the room, there's thundering applause and lots of cheers and shoulder patting. Laura had of course known about this and was not taken by surprise.

With that, the meeting dissolves into an impromptu party, sampling the latest batch of Heartland's ready to bake low-fat muffins.

CPO Best Practices

- The distinction between operational and strategic procurement needs to be managed effectively.

- In most organizations, a matrix structure that balances strategic procurement focused on categories, and operational procurement focused on geographical areas and business units, is needed.

- Trade-offs between overall corporate objectives and individual site or business unit requirements need to be addressed explicitly.

Chapter 33:
It's Not About Penny Pinching

Things are going well. We've turned the corner and now results are flowing through. The tool that shows our financial procurement performance has demonstrated that procurement can bring results to Heartland's bottom line.

However, a curious episode occurred. I'm still not sure what started it. Friday afternoon, Ross called me into his office for a meeting on short notice. Garner, our CFO, is there as well.

"Come on in, Thomas,", said Ross. "I asked Garner to join us. Hope that's okay with you."

"Sure. What would you guys like to talk about?"

Garner speaks first, "We've been taking a look at the budgets and forecasts. You know we just had month end and updated the quarterly projections."

"Yes," I said. "We've put an additional $45 million in savings into the latest update. Are you hoping to stretch that?"

"I was more focused on the departmental expenses. Yours keep going up. Your running rate on travel is three times the level we budgeted."

Taken aback, I think about how to react. Before I can say anything, Ross interjected. "No one is pointing fingers, Thomas. What Garner, what we, are saying is that we need to keep the expenses under control. It's not just in your department where the travel spending has, shall we say, gone through the roof. But yours is the clearest case. We need to deal with this."

"I hear what you're saying."

"We want to introduce stronger approvals on travel. For example, I want to mandate that departments must stay within budget on the travel line item, irrespective of savings on other budget lines. I also want all flights to be signed off by a corporate officer prior to being booked, and then countersigned by the relevant finance manager in Garner's team."

Ross paused. "That's right, Garner, isn't it. That's what we discussed?"

"Yes, it is Ross," says Garner.

"So," I said, "I could approve travel but subject to my finance manager agreeing. That sounds like an interesting process."

"There is one other thing," said Garner. "We plan to cut the current travel budgets by 50%."

"Garner wants to send a strong signal to folks. There is just too much damn travel in this organization right now."

Garner was clearly committed to this new policy. But I'm not sure how committed Ross is, or whether he was simply testing for my reaction. In any event, I needed to push back.

"I think this will cause problems—it's absolutely right that we do everything we can to minimize unnecessary travel. Whenever possible, we do videoconferences and hold voice calls across our global category and supplier teams."

"Right," said Ross.

"But, we are trying to do things differently in procurement, compared to the past. We now have genuine global category teams, and they are cross-functional. There are times when the teams need to get together to plan their approaches and develop trust and rapport. That emotional bonding can't take place purely via phone calls. Even having dinner together is a helpful process in business terms."

Garner scowled. But Ross seemed to be enjoying the conversation.

"So, Thomas, you want to fund lots of dinners and transcontinental flights, do you? How do I explain that to shareholders? It hardly sounds frugal, does it?" said Ross. His tone isn't unsympathetic though.

I could tell Ross's heart isn't really in this debate. He clearly had been egged on by Garner. I chose a subtle approach, rather than a head-on challenge. I've had enough experience in the executive corridor to know that everyone needs to save face in a debate.

"Ross, Garner, I get your point. You're absolutely right to challenge me on this. But, what I would say is that the category teams do need to travel. The big negotiations we did in Milan involved our guys from across the globe. We needed to put folks in one place to do that. Laura also needed to travel in advance to make sure that the folks in different plants understood how important it was to collect the specific data that was so crucial for success. In an ideal world it wouldn't be necessary, but you both know that the world isn't perfect and the 'personal touch' always works wonders."

"You are, as always very eloquent, Thomas," said Ross.

"The $28 million in savings are a pretty good return on the travel budget we've incurred. That's a fact, not spin. And, Ross, your trip to see the Coswalder CEO last week was important to help us for the future. We need to build the relationship so we can move forward together now that we have the right commercial terms in place. There's quite a lot of innovation on their side that we need to tap into on packaging product development, as you know. A phone call wouldn't have had the same effect as the personal touch of Ross Bailkowsky," I explain.

Even Garner was now warming to the conversation and laughed: "Now, Thomas that type of flattery is just out of order," he said. "Ross really does not need to hear that! This is an unfair negotiation."

"We hired him because he can negotiate," said Ross. "Guess we shouldn't be surprised when he does the same thing to us. Ok, Thomas, you've made some good points, we'll get back to you."

I'm pretty sure that I won that argument. There's no point in rubbing Garner's nose in it. It's best to quit while I'm ahead. I say my goodbyes and head out. I'm still not sure whether Ross was ever really serious on the travel point, or if he was just seeing how I would react. Anyway, I have other things to do.

Later on, I reflect on this little episode. On one hand, maybe I should be angry that we have delivered so much in savings and yet we then get challenged on the trivia of travel budgets. I could easily have gotten angry with Ross and Garner. Luckily, I did not. It would not have helped. I treated the conversation as a negotiation and kept calm. However, I think it has taught me a lesson. No matter how well things seem to be going, there is always potential for distractions and for colleagues to raise issues. These things just have to be managed. I recall John's exhortation to manage the present. It was good advice.

CPO Best Practices

- Recognize that the potential for distractions is ever present and needs to be managed.

- Be prepared to negotiate internally and to push back on distractions in a calm, fact-based way!

Chapter 34:
The Training Plan

I was honestly shocked and disappointed when I got the results of the skill-level assessment of our procurement people. We are about average or slightly below compared to our industry, our peer group in terms of revenue, and to companies in the regions we are in. I still remember the assessments and benchmarks we did at Autowerke. We always had a superior rating.

A training company that specializes in procurement assessments conducted the Heartland Consolidated Industries' assessment. They assessed four skill areas: analytical skills—data gathering, analysis, and modeling; procurement process skills—strategic thinking, category expertise, commercial levers, technical capabilities, negotiations, and some other cross-functional capabilities; management skills—people and project management, stakeholder management; and personal qualifications—presentation and communication skills, leadership skills, cultural awareness, and language skills.

I had different expectations for our strategic and operational buyers, and I defined what we need to have to be a best practice procurement function. I'd expected some shortcomings in language skills, especially in Europe, as most of our plants only speak the local language. In the United States with English it's a bit different, as the whole supplier market is ours. But especially in procurement skills, I'm surprised, as I had the impression that our average is above the industry average. I don't know if it is an outcome of my transformational trainings with John, but interestingly enough, my colleagues are quite well positioned in people management, stakeholder management, and cultural awareness. But the rest of the ratings come in as "weak," "poor," and so on.

Anyway, I've learned from John that I shouldn't complain, but address it instead. It's the weekend, and raining, so I start to set up a training plan; I want to address this topic soon. If I have unsolved problems, I can't relax, no matter if it is weekend, vacation, or whatever.

My goal is to train all my staff corresponding to their needs. It should be a program tailor-made to address our weaknesses.

I put the finishing touches on the Heartland Consolidated Industries Procurement Training Plan and decide to check it out with Ross. He is currently on a vacation, so I reach him by FaceTime in the Bahamas. The first thing he does is show me through his camera the beautiful view, and also the laptop that's sitting in front of him. This guy can't take vacations. He always works. It's probably not very healthy for him, but he's really full of energy. When I met him at the golf course and was offered the job, he said he only takes vacations so his wife can relax. He doesn't need vacations and is bored after two days. So I only politely ask if he has some time to chat, and he asks me what news I have for him.

"Ross, you know we did a people assessment in procurement, and the results are not very good."

He mentions that he's seen the results I forwarded to him. He laughs and says, "Thomas, I'm not used to it taking you a week to fix a problem." He smiles into the camera, but it is still hard for me to evaluate if he is joking or sincere. Probably both.

"Yes, Ross. It didn't take me more than a week to set up a professional training plan, which I would like to discuss briefly with you." Ross looks interested.

"I'd like to set up a state-of-the-art Heartland Procurement Academy, with the most recent training material and training methods that are available on the market. I would like to train all of our 300 purchasers. These purchasers should be trained in groups of 15 to 20 people to secure the learning effort. The training should take place in the regions and should also contribute to networking."

Ross answers: "So you mean something like I'm doing here. Trainings are very often seen as vacation. Sitting there for a day or two."

I interrupt: "You are perfectly right. This is why I'd like to do a different type of training plan for our procurement academy. This is a proposal of what I would like to do for the training section. We will conduct a basic training program with sourcing processes and negotiation trainings, and then more advanced training on different levers on how to reduce cost and generate value. And the new thing about it is, we will have a 30-60-90 days review." Ross is listening intently.

"What's the program, then, for the 30-60-90 days, Thomas?"

I respond that we need to work on both individual skills and also on overall group cohesion to drive common results. To this end, the regional category teams will focus in the first review on the soundness of category-specific strategy and the desired supplier relationship management; in the second review, they need a robust action plan in place; and in the third review, the first results of the focus teams should be presented. Ross likes this idea, as it is a bit different from a normal training plan that is more theoretical.

When I inform him about the potential cost, he's quite surprised that training days are so expensive, but I have a good explanation for this. "The trainers will act not only during the training classes as sparring partners and coaches for the teams, but they will jointly prepare the review meeting documents and ensure the success." I feel that he's comfortable with it, and as I have to cover it anyway from my budget, he's fine.

Ross gives advice for my, as he sees it, "technocratic" language. "Thomas, try to make the milestones more interesting for the participants. Use something like "play and familiarize" with new concepts and approaches, for the 30-day milestone, something like "do your homework" or "Seed." For the 60-day milestone, maybe "Mobilize and go for action." And for the 90-day milestone, something like "Harvest: You have your first success." Looks like Ross sometimes is on the same wavelength as John. Both of them like to use catchy words.

Great. So I will be the founder of the "Heartland Procurement Academy." I like the name. I also decide to ask John to run the team-building sessions within the program. There is nobody better qualified for this.

> | CPO Best Practices |

- The capability of the people in the function needs to be managed actively.

- Practical, goal-focused training with real work outputs is often more effective than theory-based training on concepts.

Chapter 35:
Transformed

I've become a member of Ross's innermost circle.

In the meeting with Ross, Rick, Garner and Warner, the discussion went back and forth but did not reach a decisive conclusion.

I have never seen Ross like this. For him it is either go or no go. Debating the same issue over and over again is totally out of character.

I enter the training session just as John McGrath is about to wrap up.

As you guys have observed, nurturing relationships is especially important in procurement ...

I am deeply impressed by Warner Metcalf, the chairman of the board, and his towering presence and intriguing personality.

I've found a chair next to Laura.

How is it going?

Brilliant! John is really transforming us.

It's a hot day in mid-September. The corn stands high in the fields behind our house awaiting the harvester. With the warmest weather behind us, I've extended my daily morning runs to ten miles. I'm pretty pleased with myself, but Rick thinks I'm crazy. "You're going to pay for this when you are old. Human ankles are not made for this type of permanent strain."

Privately, I agree with this, but I need the running to maintain my emotional balance. Things with Heidi have not improved and I know that time is running out. I suspect that the only reason Heidi hasn't asked for a divorce yet is that she doesn't want to repeat her sister's story. As far as I'm concerned, I really want to make our marriage work, but I'm at a total loss for what to do.

My meetings with Ross have taken an interesting turn. We hardly talk about procurement any more. For Ross, the procurement initiative is a done deal. Obviously, I see it a bit differently, since I see the huge effort people are still putting into it. But for him, things have relaxed. With six out of eight of our global category officers nominated, and the seven division procurement directors fully in tune with the initiative, I also have the bandwidth for additional topics. And Ross is doing his best to fill up all the available time I have.

Horse race: Another update

Category	Spend (in $ mn)	Savings target (in $ mn)	Category profiled	Strategy defined	Market analyzed	Execution started	Agreements negotiated	Implementation completed	Savings (in $ mn) Identified	Savings (in $ mn) Implemented
Raw materials	31,200	1,240							1,110	832
Packaging	4,800	720							842	813
Contract manufacturing	6,050	900							873	83
Logistics	4,200	630							715	715
Production equipment	2,420	360							638	638
Facilities and real estate	2,360	200							170	94
Marketing	5,950	650							677	543
General services and admin	3,070	300							234	130
Total	60,050	5,000							5,259	3,848

I've become a member of Ross's innermost circle. There's Rick, Garner, Warner Metcalf—the chairman of the board—and now me. I've just met Warner. He's an interesting guy. Growing up in the Bronx, he got into college on a football scholarship, quickly rising to become a star quarterback and playing for Indianapolis. Now he's made a fortune with real estate investments.

A few years ago he beat the incumbent congressman and served several terms. He is now shuttling between Indianapolis and Washington, DC, where he is a consultant.

Ross regularly teases Warner about becoming president of the United States. Warner typically responds with his jovial laugh and says something about his pockets not being deep enough to finance a campaign. I'm deeply impressed by Warner's towering presence and intriguing personality. And I have to admit that the prospect of talking to someone who has a chance of becoming president—he says he has considered it—puts me in awe.

With Warner spending so much time in DC, our calendars are adjusted to his availability. Today is one of those days, which means that I'll miss the first half of the training session scheduled for the Tiger group. Laura will have to chair that session, which is fine. We've divided procurement up into twenty groups encompassing people from different divisions, regions, and hierarchy levels. Each of the groups chose the name of an animal. Next to Tiger, there is Shark, Eagle, Sidewinder, Orca, Wolf, Fox, Lion, Bear, Alligator, Hornet, Wasp, Falcon, Cheetah, Gorilla, Cobra, Puma, Barracuda, Crocodile, and my personal favorite, T-Rex. I find it interesting that none of the groups selected a peaceful herbivore like an elephant. Is this a sign of being too aggressive toward the supplier? I make a mental note to discuss this with John.

In the meeting with Ross, Rick, Garner, and Warner, we discuss the potential acquisition of Meiers Milch again. That would be a bold move; Meiers Milch is twice as big as all of Heartland's dairy division combined. Meiers Milch has a dominant position in probiotic yogurts on the European market, so it would fit into Heartland's move toward more healthy products. Investors fear that the company is growing too aggressively, and they are skeptical about the growth prospects in Europe.

Today, Garner is reporting about informal talks he's had with private equity firms. There might be a chance of collaborating with one of them, which would make the deal financially easier for Heartland. "We've never done this." Ross says, "If we buy, we buy 100 percent. We know how to run the business and how to integrate it. We also know how to turn it around. Look at what Thomas and his team have achieved in procurement. Just apply our savings rate to Meiers Milch. This alone would make them a profitable business. We don't need private equity people looking over our shoulders."

"This might be our only chance to sweeten the deal for our investors," Garner replies. "And Ross, let's face it, the window of opportunity is closing. We have been pondering this idea for nearly two months now."

The discussion goes back and forth but doesn't reach a decisive conclusion. At eleven, Warner has to leave for the airport. I head for the Tiger group training and walk with Rick. "I have never seen Ross like this," Rick says. "Normally he is faster making decisions. For him it is either a go or no go. Debating the same issue over and over again is totally out of character."

"Well it would be by far the largest acquisition Heartland has ever done, right?"

"Right. And sure, Ross doesn't want to bet the company on this. But that's what I'm saying. Normally, he would simply say no and let it go."

I lack the experience with Ross in these type of decisions and I don't say anything. Privately, I'm content with my current role and don't envy Ross. I enter the training session just as John is about to wrap up.

"So let me summarize, you can't have a situation of "no relationship" with other people. There is always some type of relationship. As you guys have observed, nurturing relationships is especially important in procurement. Your internal effectiveness depends on your ability to build positive and robust relationships to people in other branches of procurement and to people in other functions."

"We have also seen that there are three ingredients to a positive relationship. These are authenticity—a difficult word—empathy, and appreciation.

"Authenticity makes you approachable. It requires you to be honest, honest to yourself, and honest to others. If you are authentic, you stand for your values and live your dream. Authenticity is risky because it means opening yourself up to others. If they recognize you for what you are, they might learn where they can hurt you. Are you ready to be authentic?"

By now I've found a chair next to Laura. "How is it going?" I whisper. "Brilliant! John is really transforming us. One of these guys even asked him for advice on how to salvage his marriage!" This jolts me back to an unwelcome dimension of my own reality. I make an effort to listen carefully to John. Maybe there's something that might help with Heidi as well.

"... and empathy also tells the other that you are taking her or him seriously. Consider who you most enjoy talking with. Are these people who listen well or people who talk a lot? Listening is harder than talking. But if you master this skill, you will never ever again get surprising reactions from your spouse, as we discussed earlier. Most misunderstandings in private affairs are caused by not listening. So, are you ready to show true empathy?"

I scan the audience. I see many serious faces nodding in agreement.

"Good. And then there is appreciation. Remember when you were a kid how your parents taught you to say "thank you"? Well that was an important lesson. Saying thank you is one of the strongest bonds we have between human beings. Unfortunately, most of us have forgotten about it. Say thank you more often, and don't take things for granted. Appreciation is most important when you disagree with someone. You can criticize the actions or the behavior of another person, but you should never criticize the other person for what she or he is. Are you ready to show appreciation more often?"

Heads nod.

"Excellent. Now remember, authenticity, empathy, and appreciation multiply, they don't add up. If one of them is zero, the quality of your entire relationship is zero. You can't compensate for a lack of empathy with lots of appreciation." He's done.

Laura gets up, thanks John, and explains that there will be a generous lunch break, and John will still be around if participants want to discuss aspects of the morning session with him. In the afternoon they will continue with a session on demand power and supply power.

While people are having lunch, John is surrounded by a large group of participants. I try to make sense of my private life. Am I authentic with Heidi? Probably. Am I showing empathy? If I'm honest with myself, this has never been my forte, and more recently, I've been a complete failure at this. Do I show appreciation? Again a clear no. John's words about saying thank you truly shocked me. Such a simple thing! When Heidi prepares dinner, I never say thank you. My immediate excuse is that I prepare dinner as often as Heidi does, so we're even, right? But no, and if I remember correctly, Heidi usually says thank you. Things are starting to spin in my head....

CPO Best Practices

- Be authentic—to your values and what you stand for.

- Be empathetic—take other people's values and needs seriously.

- Show appreciation—for the things that people do.

Chapter 36:
Professional Success and Private Disaster

Is she going to leave me? This is the question I've been asking myself for quite a long time now. The conversations I have with Heidi are largely reduced to blame games: Who was responsible for the move that is bringing bad luck to our marriage. Other things I'm blamed for are that I'm married to my job or that I have no time for the kids. Yes, I missed the school performance of *Beauty and the Beast* where Johanna was Belle. I really regret it, but it was out of my hands. Flight cancellation due to heavy fog in Milan. This led to another night in Milan, and so I missed the connecting flight to the States from Frankfurt. It is not easy being away from my family, missing my kids grow up, and feeling guilty about it. But we never had the situation before where she blames me for being away from home.

Maybe Heidi is blaming me because she has met some man here? I know she's a very attractive and charismatic woman who could easily attract men. Is she the kind of woman who is currently seeking somebody who has enough time for her? I'm sure I'm too focused on Heartland, and I have spent a majority of the past 1 ½ years on the transformation of procurement. I know men often say that they invest this time to have a good life with their family. This is exactly what I tell myself: I just want to fix the problems at Heartland, make procurement and myself successful, and afterward have a regular life with my kids and my wife. But now it looks like I've fixed most of the problems in my professional life. Perhaps I need to learn some lessons now in my private life. While I'm thinking about how I will miss Heidi, the time spent together with her, her smile, falling asleep, waking up together, and the vacations together, my telephone rings.

I can't believe it: It's Frank Kalligan—the chief editor of *Global Economy*. I've never met him in person, but I have read many of his articles. He is a brilliant writer, a sharp thinker, extremely critical, and a genius with his economic outlooks for companies. So why is he calling me? He quickly introduces himself: "Frank Kalligan. I work for *The Global Economy*." He asks me if I have some time and starts with a question on the status of the announced $5 billion savings that Heartland Consolidated Industries procurement 12 months ago. My first impression is that this guy has an arrogant voice. Funny thing is, after I answer his question with "we have currently implemented $4.5 billion," he immediately changes his tone.

"Thomas," he says, "this is a truly a great achievement. I heard rumors recently that Heartland is very successful in its procurement transformation, and given the fact that you have already nearly reached the target, I would like to put Heartland and you on the cover of our magazine. Do you think that you could fit a meeting into your agenda for an interview?"

I don't know what to say or how to hide my excitement. "Frank, it's difficult this week, but what about next week—Tuesday for lunch at Heartland?"

At Heartland we have our normal cafeteria and then a special restaurant for important corporate guests and clients. This is where we meet. Of course, I prepared myself over the weekend for the interview, thinking through some key questions that Frank could have.

We start our lunch and the first question is, as expected, about where we stand with Heartland's transformation program and the financial benefits. Great, I've prepared for this question: "Our transformation is proceeding quite well, but we aren't finished yet. Heartland started with the procurement transformation's program about 12 months ago, and we think that all in all we need about 24 months to make our achievements truly sustainable. The financial benefit is going well: out of the $5 billion savings we had as our target, we've already implemented $4.5 billion and—here's something new—we will not stop at $5 billion. Our procurement team set itself a new target of $6 billion in savings," I answer. "That's why it will take another year."

He digs more into details about our transformation: "So is what you call procurement transformation not just another savings project? And isn't it completed when the savings are achieved?"

"No. Procurement transformation is much more than achieving savings. Savings are a kind of catalyst for the transformation. Procurement transformation is seeking internal and external effectiveness. This means effectiveness within the organization—close collaboration within procurement, but also cross-functional collaboration with other departments. External effectiveness means that you find the most appropriate strategies with your suppliers. Having achieved both means that you are a 'procurement champion.' We've managed to achieve more than 80% of our goals in terms of external effectiveness and about half of our goals on internal effectiveness. It is not enough to draw new organizational charts or processes. People have to use new processes, and this does not happen from one day to the next. To become a procurement champion, you need to have thought leadership in content, but it is not enough to have the best tools, methodologies, and approaches. People matter a lot, and this is one of the key success factors. Win the hearts and minds of people!"

He wants to know the main success factors, especially the softer, or people-focused, side. I find it interesting that the *Global Economy* is so interested in it, but I'm well prepared for this question.

"We at Heartland Consolidated Industries, in my opinion, had five very important success factors on the soft side. These are:

(1) Lead the transformation: We have had, with our CEO Ross Bailkowsky, a leader who fully supported the transformation. Ross has provided during the last 12 months the resources I needed. He removed the obstacles, was committed, and took over personal accountability for the procurement's success. He said, right in the beginning, 'Tell me who you need to achieve the goal of having a best-in-class procurement function and I will make them available for you.'

"**(2) Create a case for change:** We have had, again, right from the beginning, a compelling and logical case for change. There was the clear goal announced by Ross save $5 billion. He also announced it publicly. The goal was communicated clearly, and everyone in the organization understood that this was necessary. As we were facing some problems, there was also an intrinsic and personal case for change for every employee in that they saw the opportunity to maintain their jobs as well as to not lose parts of their salaries. Even if it is a bit selfish, saving money on the back of suppliers was more motivating for them than having to adapt their lifestyle owing to job loss. The more positive part of the case for change for my colleagues at Heartland was that I offered a vision that we become as professional as the procurement organization at my former employer Autowerke. The guys just saw the need to have a reputation that—just like at Autowerke—Heartland procurement is best-in-class, and companies are seeking to hire people from Heartland. This was something that made my people proud and motivated them.

"**(3) Mobilize stakeholders:** I still remember my first fights and also the problems I faced at Heartland with our international procurement organization, but especially with other departments. I do not want to name these departments. Until that point in time, I did not believe that even top managers could be so averse to change. No one liked to leave their comfort zone or change the way of working together with procurement. Especially because all of a sudden, procurement also wanted to contribute to innovation, in product style and other areas. Before, this was just not accepted by other departments. But also in procurement, I was seen as 'just an automotive guy not knowing the foods and retail business.' I was told many times that only extended relationships with long-time suppliers are possible in this industry. I brought all the important stakeholders together and we did a workshop on transformation. In this workshop we discussed what the comfort zone means—it is comfortable, but it will not make us successful over the long run. I said we needed to enter the learning zone. This means change. When we discussed examples in which even market leaders met their demise within their comfort zone, we got stakeholders really mobilized.

"**(4) Motivate people:** I have to admit, nothing motivates people more than success. Celebrating the big victories—such as the first $20 million savings or the first big idea that works—and identifying the 'stars' in the organization kept the momentum going. I still remember the celebrations for our first $100 million savings. The first billion—and I have to underline that these were savings certified by our CFO—was a big party. Ross gave a speech honoring the results and brought some of the key contributors to the front line at this party, but he also mentioned that we had not yet reached the goal. Procurement people, production people, but also our engineers, were present and were named as key contributors. I remember one of my team members, a young professional from Italy presenting her work and achievements in front of the board. This was 8 months ago, and she was appointed as our first global category officer—not only was this great for her, but it is also a very good sign for the company. Many people say you cannot motivate with money. That's probably true, but at least at Heartland people were extremely happy (and also motivated) when they received an extra bonus for contributing to the project.

"**(5) Train people:** We did a lot of training. Of course, there were procurement-related, on-the-job, and off-the-job trainings, such as sessions on strategic sourcing processes or negotiation skills. We also did innovation workshops with suppliers. This was also more of the content part of trainings than you would find everywhere. But we also did training on human or emotional topics. This is extremely important—to instruct people on how to focus on those things they can influence and let go of the rest. We did training on emotional topics—regarded probably as unprofessional in the past, but we have seen that it is key to really transforming a company like Heartland."

When Frank tells me that he never thought Heartland Consolidated Industries was such a "soft-focused" company, I tell him that the soft topics are needed to make hard topics sustainable. So they are probably not just soft esoteric things that nobody needs, but an integral part of business and transformation success.

I'm quite exhausted after the interview, and a bit nervous about what will really be published, as only a few quotes will be included. I also won't have a chance to see the article beforehand. But I'm quite proud that the *Global Economy* is interested in Heartland's procurement transformation story.

I and the group fixed most of the problems—and now I also have to fix the personal problems with my wife, whom I love.

Not knowing the answer there, I call John and ask him about his advice regarding private life. He has been the key for transformation success at Heartland, so I'm hopeful that he can help transform my marriage. When I reach John—he is of course on his boat—and ask him, he answers that I know everything I need to know, and reminds me of these things once again: "Remember the talk on authenticity, empathy, and appreciation, Thomas?" He ends our conversation by saying, "humans are humans."

Just as I finish up my call with John, I see that there are missed calls on my mobile and another caller is on the phone. It's one of these headhunters asking me if I'd be interested in new challenges again. They've been calling a lot these last couple weeks. If I recall correctly, it started when we issued a press release that announced Heartland's financial results and the role procurement played in them. I don't talk with the headhunters, as I don't consider my goal finished yet. I'll reconsider in 18 months, but my place right now is to be CPO at Heartland. I want to complete the transformation. And it is not yet stable enough to leave behind. The only thing I don't refuse to do is to be guest speaker at Harvard on procurement. I'm really proud of this offer and think it is also important to put procurement into the discussion at high caliber universities as well.

Chapter 37:
Rewarded

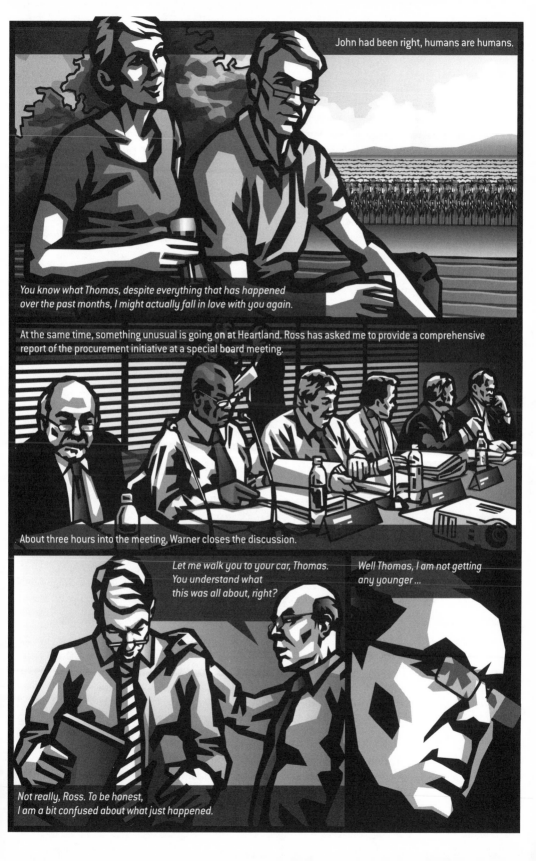

John was right, humans are humans. The means to fix things with Heidi have always been available to me. What John had outlined didn't just apply to the corporate environment, but also to my home life. Authenticity, empathy, and appreciation are the key. Again, I'd taken too much for granted. Being close to the precipice of our relationship, I've finally managed to change the course. It starts with actively listening to what Heidi has to say. I return to the dinner table after putting the kids to bed and asking Heidi how her day was.

Initially, she's skeptical. "Don't you have work to do?" and "Where are your gadgets? Normally, I can't talk to you for more than two minutes before you start checking your e-mails." But I persist. After a couple of days, Heidi lets her guard down and starts to enjoy our regular conversations. I avoid taking the easy way out of tricky topics. I take my time before answering and remain true to myself.

Showing appreciation remains the hardest for me. When we have fights—and of course we still have fights—I'm struggling to limit my critique to actions and avoiding getting personal. This is made harder by the fact that Heidi doesn't play by my rules because she is unaware of them. I ponder sharing the insights I've gained with Heidi, but then shy away from it. Let's face it; I'm not Heidi's guru. I am the last person to sell a recipe to her on how to treat me. I've applied another John lesson instead: "The most effective way to change the way a person treats you is to treat that person the way you want to be treated." So I hang on, stubbornly enduring setback after setback and, gradually, things improve. One evening, when we're sitting on the enclosed porch, looking out over the cornfields, sipping a glass of red wine, Heidi says half-jokingly, "You know what Thomas, despite everything that has happened over the past few months, I can see how hard you are trying to mend our relationship. And it's working. I might actually fall in love with you again."

At the same time, something unusual is going on at Heartland. Ross has asked me to provide a comprehensive report of the procurement initiative at a special board meeting. All executive and non-executive board members will be there, and the only agenda topic I'm aware of is my speech. Rick, who is still far better connected than I am, also can't make sense of it. Rick has conceded that he can't recall that type of board meeting.

After giving it a second thought, I go to see Ross to better understand the background of the meeting, and to get hints on how to prepare for it. The response I get doesn't really help. He says I should provide a summary about what's happened the past year and half, and be ready for a discussion. Not wanting to disappoint anyone, I pay extra attention to the preparation of my speech. I look at all the slides I've ever used at Heartland and even some I brought over from Autowerke. After many drafts, I'm finally satisfied with the result. My usually preferred approach is to go mostly with free speech, but I write a script for the entire speech and rehearse it several times.

This thorough preparation and the fact that I consider myself to be an experienced speaker gives me a lot of confidence when I enter the room. There is an air of expectation and excitement in the room that I can't place anywhere. After a brief and cordial introduction by Warner, I deliver my speech largely interrupted. So far, my diligent preparation has helped, but what I wasn't prepared for were the questions they asked. They were mostly addressing the span across most of Heartland's business, and not just procurement. The board members seemed to be especially interested in my ideas and opinions about boosting revenues and gross margin. About three hours into the meeting, Warner closes the discussion.

"Thomas, you may wonder why we wanted to see you and what the background to all our questions is. I am not in a position to disclose everything to you yet. At a high level, we are debating reshuffling things at Heartland in a way that would allow Ross to focus more on the big picture and on the strategic direction we are taking. The purpose of today's meeting was to see what role you can play in this. Needless to say, this should be kept confidential. Give us a couple of days and we will get back to you with more."

Warner announces a half hour coffee break and dismisses me. On the way out, Ross puts his heavy hand on my shoulder.

"Let me walk you to your car Thomas. You understand what this was all about, right?"

"Not really, Ross. To be honest, I am a bit confused about what just happened."

"Well Thomas, I'm not getting any younger. The board has been pushing me toward succession planning for years now. They considered none of the executives around here to be up for the job. Don't get me wrong, Rick and the guys are good people, but they would merely continue the status quo. But Heartland has to change and become a contemporary player in the world. We also didn't want to bring in a COO from another company or a CEO from a smaller player. I never really liked lateral hires. You know what they say, to a man with a hammer, everything looks like a nail. When I met you on that flight we had, I had this immediate gut feeling that there was and is something special about you. Obviously, you needed to grow. But what you have accomplished over the past 18 months was an impressive feat. I want you to become the COO of Heartland with all the functions and divisions reporting to you."

"Wow, Ross, I don't know what to say, I'm speechless."

"Take your time to digest. Anyway it is not official yet, and we need to go through a couple of formalities before we can announce it."

Chapter 38:
The Heart Attack

After a very successful meeting about the extraordinary results in the last financial year, Ross had a heart attack.

We dial 9-1-1 and an ambulance comes within 10 minutes. They take him to Fort Wayne's hospital

The hospital mentions that he will have to stay, if everything goes well, for at least four weeks, and then has to go to a rehabilitation resort to relax. Ross's wife stays with him all the time.

After only 4 hours, I get up to be at the office early.

Telling Heidi about Ross's heart attack brings her to tears. She immediately takes my hands and hugs me.

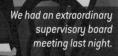

We had an extraordinary supervisory board meeting last night.

Thomas, congratulations. If you accept, you will be the interim CEO.

He always joked that he will die in the office and they'll have to carry him out of Heartland's office building—and now it is almost true? I'm calling the hospital again to get the latest news on Ross's condition. This morning, after a very successful meeting about the extraordinary results in the last financial year, Ross had a heart attack while drinking a glass of Champagne with us and the other board members. We were celebrating the best result that Heartland Consolidated Industries has ever had—despite the problems that we were facing.

I admit that I'm a bit proud especially since procurement contributed the most to this result. Even I know that the financial results of a company are a common success, but this year's EBIT is clearly higher due to procurement. There will also be a section in Heartland's annual report about procurement, what it's achieved, our supplier relationship management, and some other aspects. We will even have an explanation of the procurement performance figure Heartland has achieved and what the figure means. This is clearly becoming more and more important with analysts.

So right as we raise our glasses, he feels a bit weak in the knees and has to sit down: He still tries to manage the situation and says that these fabulous figures should not only make him, but everybody, a bit weak in the knees. When he suddenly takes his hand, tries to open his tie, and then takes hold of his heart with his hand, everybody knows this is a heart attack.

We dial 9-1-1 and an ambulance comes within 10 minutes. They take him to Fort Wayne's hospital and Dr. Nessler, one of the most famous heart specialists in the United States, takes care of him and saves his life—at least for the moment. Nobody knows what's happening over the next few hours and days.

It's quite strange knowing that the mentor, who was always there for me, who was backing everything I did and planned, is not here anymore, at least for the moment. The hospital mentions that he will have to stay, if everything goes well, for at least four weeks, and then has to go to a rehabilitation resort to relax. Ross's wife stays with him all the time. It is really heartwarming to see them together and the love that is still between them. Ross always worked a lot, but his wife is always his first priority.

Ross is not only a good mentor, but also a real role model of being successful in the job, managing problems, and also being successful at home. Telling Heidi about Ross's heart attack brings her to tears. She immediately takes my hands and hugs me. I've never seen Heidi this sad and deeply depressed. She still has both of her parents, and has never had to deal with fatal diseases or death. When she stops crying and is able to speak again, she mentions that it has to be so hard to lose or even nearly lose a person you love. She mentions that in this situation everybody will regret not having spent more time with him, time dedicated to nice moments, and relatedly, perhaps not having been able getting to know the real personality and concerns of your partner.

We talk for a long time. Heidi and I are going through our photo albums of our first weekend, first holiday together, our marriage, the birth of our kids, holidays together … but also the birthday parties of the kids I missed because of work or travel. I realize in this moment how important family is and how important my life is with Heidi. I also begin to think about my priorities. Whenever somebody asked me, I always said, my family and my wife. But do I really live like that? Don't I always put my job, my company, my career in first place? Whenever I had important business meetings, it was always my family that got second place. I never said that I'm not cancelling my holidays because my family needs me—I did the contrary and said that my family has to understand that I have to cancel. Well, for my career it was probably the right thing to do, but I need to reconsider a bit for the future. At 2 a.m., we finish our tea. Despite this very tragic situation, I feel so close to Heidi.

After only 4 hours, I get up to be at the office early. Since Ross won't be there, I feel a bit responsible to "take care" of Heartland. The time of absence should not worry Ross too much, because he knows the executives and board members will continue to deliver excellent performance.

Warner's large, dark blue Bentley is already in front of the door and a note on my desk says that I should call him immediately. When I call, he asks me into his office. After some questions about my work as CPO and the transformation I'm doing, he starts to speak about the purpose for my being there: "We had an extraordinary supervisory board meeting yesterday night and talked about how we are going to lead Heartland over the coming months and who should become interim CEO. We discussed several options. Thomas, you are not the one who has the longest tenure within Heartland. You are also not the one who went through different jobs within Heartland, and you are also not the one who is most connected in Fort Wayne compared to your peers." Why can't Warner just say who will be my boss for the coming months until Ross's comeback. He continues: "But you are the most connected person within Heartland, you have the trust of people, you proved that you are able to deliver results in difficult situations, and you are able to transform people. Thomas, congratulations. If you accept, you will be the interim CEO." He smiles and I immediately respond "Yes," while thinking about Ross and knowing that this is probably what he wants.

Chapter 39:
Looking Into the Future

Fortune smiles on Ross. He recovers.
A week after his heart attack, I was told that Ross held
a private meeting at his home with Warner to discuss the future.

*Ross, this isn't easy for me, but I have to be plain.
The company cannot have an interim CEO for too long.*

*You're right, Warner. It would be great if Thomas could
be confirmed in his role.*

Ross and his wife had, indeed, already agreed that
now was the right moment to step down and make a
complete life change.

The board held another extraordinary meeting that week, and I was confirmed as the new CEO.
Ross agreed to stay on as a director.
His vast experience of Heartland will be useful for the company.

Fortune smiles on Ross. He recovers from his heart attack. His doctors say he has to recuperate and can return to work gradually over the following 12 weeks. They also advise him to change his lifestyle. Ross has always enjoyed the good things in life—including exquisite food and drink. This will have to change. The stress of managing Heartland Consolidated Industries has also taken its toll on him. He's now in his early sixties.

A week after his heart attack, I was told that Ross held a private meeting at his home with Warner to discuss the future. Warner was supportive, but he has discussed the situation with his fellow non-executive directors. Warner got down to business:

"Ross, this isn't easy for me, but I have to be plain. You know it will be hard for you to carry on after this," he said. "We think that you may need a while to recuperate. The company cannot have an interim CEO for too long."

Warner was expecting a fight, or at least a counterargument. Instead, Ross simply said, "You're right, Warner. I think now is the moment to hand it over to the younger generation. It would be great if Thomas could be confirmed in his role. I think he will do a great job." Ross and his wife have already agreed that now is the right moment to step down and make a life change. The heart attack has been a warning that Ross decided he should heed. He agreed to stay on as a director. His vast experience of Heartland will be useful for the company.

The board held another extraordinary meeting that week, and I was confirmed as the new CEO. While I genuinely regret the circumstances that brought me here, good fortune has certainly smiled on me. I'm the first CEO of Heartland from a procurement background: the previous routes to the top job have invariably been from a consumer marketing background. I know that I still have a lot to learn.

At home, the day my appointment is announced, I ponder my situation. I think about the advice John's given me. I also think about the lessons I've learned as CPO and how I will use them.

I'll now need to achieve results more than ever through motivating and encouraging people to perform—all 55,000 of them, in fact. I'll have to empower my team and offer the right guidance and support to enable them to deliver results. If I try to do too much and control everything, it won't work. On top of that, I'll no doubt risk losing my marriage a second time. I realize that this matters much more than being CEO. As I'm thinking, Heidi steps into the room. We look at each other. I say, "You matter much more to me than this new job. You do realize that, don't you?"

Heidi smiles and says, "I know that, Thomas."

Postscript

Thomas has now settled into the new role as CEO.

Heartland Consolidated Industries is flourishing as a business.

Laura has succeeded Thomas as the CPO.

The procurement function continues to grow.

Thomas and Heidi are still very much together.

Thomas and John continue to meet up on the boat every couple of months. Ross now joins whenever he can too. He finds it therapeutic. The three of them discuss sailing, the challenges of running a global corporation, and how to make relationships work.

Dear Reader,

We hope that you enjoyed reading the book as much as we enjoyed writing it. Should you be interested in receiving a free booklet with more information on the concepts, approaches and tools Thomas Sutter applied in his journey to transform procurement at Heartland Consolidated Industries Inc., please register at: www.thecpo.net

Yours sincerely,

Christian Schuh
Stephen Easton
Michael Strohmer
Armin Scharlach
Peter Scharbert